65761

DATE			

William Everson

THE CROOKED LINES OF GOD
A Trilogy

*

The Residual Years
The Veritable Years
The Integral Years

by William Everson

VERSE

These Are the Ravens (1935)
San Joaquin (1939)
The Masculine Dead (1942)
The Waldport Poems (1944)
War Elegies (1944)
The Residual Years (1944)
Poems MCMXLII (1945)
The Residual Years (1948)
A Privacy of Speech (1949)
Triptych for the Living (1951)
An Age Insurgent (1959)
The Crooked Lines of God (1959)
The Year's Declension (1961)
The Hazards of Holiness (1962)
The Poet is Dead (1964)
The Blowing of the Seed (1966)
Single Source (1966)
The Rose of Solitude (1967)
In the Fictive Wish (1967)
A Canticle to the Waterbirds (1968)
The Springing of the Blade (1968)
The Residual Years (1968)
The City Does not Die (1969)
The Last Crusade (1969)
Who is She That Looketh Forth As the Morning (1972)
Tendril in the Mesh (1973)
Black Hills (1973)
Man-Fate (1974)
River-Root/A Syzygy (1976)
The Mate-Flight of Eagles (1977)
Rattlesnake August (1978)
The Veritable Years (1978)

PROSE

Robinson Jeffers: Fragments of an Older Fury (1968)
Archetype West: The Pacific Coast as a Literary Region (1976)

WILLIAM EVERSON

The VERITABLE YEARS 1949-1966

With an Afterword

by

ALBERT GELPI

Santa Barbara

BLACK SPARROW PRESS

1978

LIBRARY OF CONGRESS CATALOGING IN PUBLICATION DATA

Everson, William, 1912-
  The veritable years, 1949-1966.

  (His The crooked lines of God ; 2)
  I. Title. II. Series.
PS3509.V65A6   1968 vol. 2   78-18183
ISBN 0-87685-379-3
ISBN 0-87685-378-5 pbk.
ISBN 0-87685-380-7 signed

for Mary Fabilli

TABLE OF CONTENTS

PREFACE

In retrospect my life emerges as a kind of Californian odyssey—an odyssey in the sense that every life is a mythic journey through time; and Californian in the sense that the scale of the American West casts its presence over the scenario of quest, determining the broader ethos within which the ideological progression is enacted. This progression involves three basic levels, making a trilogy of the work achieved, each volume bearing the stamp of its own spiritual emphasis, while retaining the larger regional impress of its origin: the spirit of place.

The first part, from my early twenties to mid-thirties, is dominated by Nature. Growing up in the San Joaquin Valley, I married, wrote my books and planted a vineyard, launching out on the vocation of farmer-poet— then lost it all in World War II when I refused military service and was sent to the Oregon coast as a conscientious objector. At War's end I returned to California with empty hands, but rather than reenter the Valley I settled in the San Francisco Bay area. A deepening center of gravity was focussing within the context of another place.

The poetry of this first interval was published as *The Residual Years* (New Directions, 1948), so called because it suggests a man's early phase of life when he engages the residue of history, struggling to discover his personal identity against the weight of human precedent (his deep heredity, his broad environment)—everything that comes down as the legacy of the past.

The second part, from my mid-thirties into my fifties, was dominated by God, and stands in antithetical relationship to the first. I have called the work of this period *The Veritable Years* because it represents a man's attempt to break the residual power of the past, achieve union with a metaphysical Absolute possessing intrinsic veritability on its own terms, beyond the power of process. Embracing Catholicism, I withdrew from the world, first on a grant which providentially arrived at that moment, then with the Catholic Worker movement in the slums of Oakland, finally to enter monastic life in the Dominican Order. Receiving the name of Brother Antoninus, I served for eighteen years as a lay monk, completing the body of verse which is here presented.

As I look back on this volume from the distance of a dozen years it is apparent that it traces a certain radical psychic contour. It began with a violent break from the past: almost nothing in *The Residual Years* prepares for it. Whereas that book was largely horizontal in emphasis, this one is emphatically vertical. Imagine a compass with the North-South directions representing opposed psychic polarities, the Spirit and the Flesh. Think of a life set toward the extreme vertical, the Magnetic Pole of God, the True North. In the beginning, the conversion moment, the needle has shot upright, and through the first section has remained there. With the second section it begins to edge down ever so slightly, then with increasing momentum, toward the horizontal. Here occurs a two and a half year hiatus, actually the hidden breakover point of the volume. For with "River-Root" the needle plummets downward. But in section four, "The Hazards of Holiness," resistance sets in, and the tension created generates a new phase of the spiritual ordeal called The Dark Night of the Soul. Finally, in "The Rose of Solitude," an equilibrium is sought, and for a time held in painful equipoise, only to collapse at the close, leaving the needle fluttering erratically, seeking support.

The third part of my life, from my mid-fifties on, attempts a resolution. Its poetry will be called *The Integral Years*, representing a man's effort to integrate into a synthetic whole the dichotomies that have split him, the thesis and antithesis that divide the world. Its opening note has already been struck in the single volume *Man-Fate* (1974) wherein the compass needle has plunged below the horizontal to be drenched in the flesh, blindly seeking another course. The line of quest, however, is not yet established.

As a general title for the trilogy I have chosen *The Crooked Lines of God*, after the famous Portuguese proverb "God writes straight with crooked lines." It preserves the fundamentally religious orientation of everything I have attempted, while accenting the inexplicable reversals that have so painfully complicated my life. As a short title, too, *Crooked Lines* suggests the irregular versification, my own sense of angularity and torsion as the shaping power in poetry.

Taken as a whole, the trilogy might be said to trace the ancient mythological journey, an amplification of the archetype represented in all rites of passage: *separation-initiation-return*. The first two lives now stand behind me as realized, and the final, inclusive one is well begun. But what it brings rests with the future's stark imperatives: the mystery of time, the power of my soul, and the providence of God.

In conclusion I can do no better than quote my foreword to the original 1959 appearance of the poems here presented as the opening section. If it exasperated critics then, annoyed that any author should adopt so morbidly self-indulgent an attitude toward what he has done, it yet was the way this one saw himself midway in his journey. A man wrestling first with God then with his own shadow, sometimes confusing them, generates a strange and fitful light, a lurid apocalyptic glare. In any case it will serve to introduce the reader to the psychic world he is about to enter:

God writes straight. My crooked lines, tortured between grace and the depraved human heart (my heart), gouge out the screed of my defection. Everywhere about me the straight writing hems me in, compresses me, flattens my will. I write crooked. Error after error blows through me, the corruptible mortal man, whose every gesture reeks of imperfection. Would you have it straight? I am not God. The matchless God-writing, calligraphed unendingly on trees, peaks, rivers, oceans, lakes, rebukes and dazzles me. I must hush my heart . . .

The Divine Writing goes forward with an excoriate straightness, but never in the manner one supposes; nor does it ever relate precisely what one hopes to hear. I have written, but what I have written is undone, not done. I have labored to make a birth of my life, but it becomes, in retrospect, only a long crooked line. This much, however, I do know; and given the nature of Reality it cannot be otherwise: all my violations, virulent as they are, in the end can only make for the good. My evil cannot win out. I wrote; I have written; I will write. But no matter how crooked I set it down, God writes it straight.

If I do not experience today either the intense religious passion or the consequent inner travail that went into these words, still, I know there must somehow be kept alive in my being the ineluctable tension between the goodness of God and my own evil, which shape between them the core of man's conscience. If I forget that, what is worth remembering?

W. E.

Ash Wednesday, 1978
Kingfisher Flat
Swanton, California

PROLOGUE:
AT THE EDGE

Let not the tempest of water drown me, nor the
deep swallow me up:
And let not the pit shut her mouth upon me.

—PSALM LXVII

There is a mark, made on the soul in its first wrong doing, and
    that is a taint.
And the mark of that taint either widens or wanes:
As the soul decrees in its inclination so will it be.
For this world is the place wherein the pureborn soul creates its
    destiny.
It becomes, at body's death, all it has tended to make of itself:
    that which it wishes to be.

So will it be seen, that there is no necessity of this life,
No hurt nor harshness, that may, in the consideration of the
    soul,
Assume precedence over the decisiveness of that final end.
For its hurts and harshnesses are not permanent things.
They are as tests. Their use is a way of working on that soul,
So it may truly determine its preferment, what it intends to do.
Whereas the ending is an absolute, an absolute as dense as the
    immutable past,
As irrevocable as the moment just gone, and now forever
    assumed into the majestic finality of the past of time.
For the ending act is the soul's last choice, in which it declares
    itself,
Which is, for the most, the totality of its choices in the determi-
    nation of its end.
Save this: that even upon finality, if it has done ill in the choices
    of its life, it is not yet too late.

Not until death drives it over the edge is it ever too late.
But still it may, by a great thrust of the will, a wrench so
    fraught with contrition,
The split pain of guilt self-owned, acknowledged and deplored;
And in the blaze of that knowledge sees to itself, a thing so
    frightful to its sudden sight,
Fungoid, so spongy with sloth and the foulnesses of its use,
That in dread it recoils, and from the grasp of fiends, screeching,
    hurls itself out—
Only, at that hour, into such a stabbing of the heart, may the
    Word move and redeem.

Rare! Rare at the final! Rare at the last!
Too soft, too easy and too slack is the self-willed soul,
That never in its time made move to right itself. It goes into its
    death
Bearing the debilitate burden of its ease, which is the ease only
    of the usage of this world.
And like a coffin at sea, weighted, and the weights are its sins,
It swings out, tips forward, drops, and sinks fast down into the
    body of the Sea of Death, which is the Hell,
And the weights of the coffin take it rapidly down to that
    scrupulous mark
Where the drag of the sin and the buoyant lift of the mercy of
    God,
Hang in exquisite balance—there does it sustain, suspended.
And it will never float.

                Nor will it ever seek to.
For whoever in life has rejected God will never in death desire
    Him.
For over the Ocean of Death shines the great ambient light of
    the Lord, which is pure,
Which is the totality of all the impelling pureness the soul had
    rejected in life.

And as that soul in life preferred the darkness of sin to the
purity of light,
So in the depths of the Sea of Death will that soul prefer the
darkness of death.
For to be drawn to the surface of the Sea of Death and in the
open light,
Which everywhere on the islands of the Sea of Death glitters
and gleams;
And to have that coffin opened up to the Eye of Day; and to have
the thing therein which it is,
Which it has made of itself, which it has created of itself;
That thing, rotten with slime and the slimy bone;
To have that thing of the self revealed to the very Eye of
Day—No, that it would never do.
But rather would hang down there in the grim balance,
Crushed under the tons of the weight of the Waters of Death,
Where those sea-monsters, who are its masters now, attend it.
There does it suffer and suffice, and has its way,
Which is the way of death, and constitutes
The sufficiency of death; which is the terrible
Contentment of the damned.

THE VERITABLE YEARS
1949-1966

BOOK ONE:
THE CROOKED LINES OF GOD
1949

God writes straight with crooked lines . . .

—PORTUGUESE PROVERB

TRIPTYCH FOR THE LIVING

I. THE UNCOUTH

And there were in the same country shepherds watching and keeping the nightwatches . . .

A mild autumn, rain, and the high pastures
Greened again with good verdure. But at solstice
Wind northed for cold, and they brought out the sheep:
Nights crippling, frost in the hollows at dawn,
The wind blowing as out of the depths of a void,
Blowing as out of the nethermost places of earth.
And on the third day, near dusk,
Being come at last to the wilderness edge,
Drew in their flocks, made nightfall there, the sheepherders;
Built weedfire; would go next day
Down to the valley, warm,
To the sheltered fields, the snug
Sequestered folds: a more tolerant winter.

For the sheep only. As for them, the herdsmen,
They'd rather hug out the year on a juniper ridge
Than enter now, where the hard-bitten settlers
Fenced their acres; where the merchants
Wheedled the meager gain of summer;
Where the brindled mastiffs
Mauled the wethers. For the sheep were hated;
Themselves were hated; their ways were of sheep;
They wore rough skins of sheep;
And the stink of the sheep
Hung everywhere about them.

And they made their weedfire,
Gravely; this for them was the last night.
Tomorrow was the world's,

And the world disdained them.
They had no knowledge of the world.

Nor had they knowledge as yet of the Angel.

For these faces were fated.
The fire, in its fletch and dapple,
Fretted the countenance of a humanity
That had demonstrated only the crude capacity to survive;
The brows hardly clefted by thought,
Where hope, as on the face of the ram,
Never had recourse. Something there was about to happen,
As if a soul were to be bestowed,
Where the naked intelligence,
That prime, animal aptitude for life,
Retained its purity.

And the world, of whom these the uncouth were most despised,
Mocked off the streets to keep the cold nightwatches there
Over the wilderness-hearted earth,
Dreamed blindly on of the transforming grace
These were now to receive.

II. THE COMING

> And she brought forth her firstborn son and wrapped him up
> in swaddling bands and laid him in a manger . . .

Blood, and the black
Bull-trodden earth, where the cow
Had bled of the womb-blind calf,
Where the shuddering ewe
Had bled, in the beast's
Fortuity, the beast's
Groan.

It too, it also: birth,
Like death, ravenous—
An unspeakable rank fertility of earth
Splitting its pod—
But this time a difference.
That lull in the air, that lapse!
As if the great device of the flesh,
The need of the flesh
Made flesh, the flesh
Founded forever upon the flesh,
Blood on the blood—
As if, on the instant, the stroke were checked,
And the flame sprang through,
Purely, between the forces of the pang,
Hued with the flush of Godhead,
Set round with the tongues of angels,
Burning and flashing
In the strewn litter
On the somber floor.

Nor would that night contain it.
There was an age, insurgent,
Scrawled on the stonework of the temple wall.
There was the massive aftermath,
Flanked with the doom of kings,
And the secret seed
Spored in the bowels of Empire.
There was the powerful regrouping of the mind,
Where the sotted puppets
Snored on their grosser thrones.
That. And the bare power,
Which is love, forged now, in the frighted human soul,
As the force of a love, larger than it,
Swells the wizened heart
To the stature of a faith.

Birth, like death,
Transcended. The blood
Burned out of the stable floor.
Outside, the oxen and the ass
Crunch their corn. But the man!
The man! seized in that vortex
Breaks on his knees
And prays!

III. THE WISE

Behold, there came wise men from the East to Jerusalem, saying
Where is He . . .?

Miles across the turbulent kingdoms
They came for it, but that was nothing;
That was the least. Drunk with vision,
Rain stringing the ragged beards,
When a beast lamed they caught up another
And goaded west.

For the time was on them.
Once, as it may, in the life of a man;
Once, as it was, in the life of mankind,
All is corrected. And their years of pursuit,
Raw-eyed reading the wrong texts,
Charting the doubtful calculations—
Those nights knotted with thought,
When dawn held off, and the rooster
Rattled the leaves with his blind assertion—
All that, they regarded, under the Sign,
No longer as search but as preparation.
For when the mark was made *they* saw it.
Nor stopped to reckon the fallible years,
But rejoiced and followed,

And are called wise, who learned that Truth,
When sought and at last seen,
Is never found. It is given.

And they brought their camels
Breakneck into that village,
And flung themselves down in the dung and dirt of that place,
And kissed that ground, and the tears
Ran on the face where the rain had.

THE FLIGHT IN THE DESERT

The last settlement scraggled out with a barbwire fence
And fell from sight. They crossed coyote country:
Mesquite, sage, the bunchgrass knotted in patches;
And there the prairie dog yapped in the valley;
And on the high plateau the short-armed badger
Delved his clay. But beyond that the desert,
Raw, unslakable, its perjured dominion wholly contained
In the sun's remorseless mandate, where the dim trail
Died ahead in the watery horizon: God knows where.

And there the failures: skull of the ox,
Where the animal terror trembled on in the hollowed eyes;
The catastrophic wheel, split, sandbedded;
And the sad jawbone of a horse. These the denials
Of the retributive tribes, fiercer than pestilence,
Whose scrupulous realm this was.

Only the burro took no notice: the forefoot
Placed with the nice particularity of one
To whom the evil of the day is wholly sufficient.
Even the jocular ears marked time.

But they, the man and the anxious woman,
Who stared pinch-eyed into the settling sun,
They went forward into its denseness
All apprehensive, and would many a time have turned
But for what they carried. That brought them on.
In the gritty blanket they bore the world's great risk,
And knew it; and kept it covered, near to the blind heart,
That hugs in a bad hour its sweetest need,
Possessed against the drawn night
That comes now, over the dead arroyos,
Cold and acrid and black.

This was the first of his goings forth into the wilderness of the
    world.
There was much to follow: much of portent, much of dread.
But what was so meek then and so mere, so slight and strengthless,
(Too tender, almost, to be touched)—what they nervously guarded
Guarded them. As we, each day, from the lifted chalice,
That fragile Bread the mildest tongue subsumes,
To be taken out in the blatant kingdom,
Where Herod sweats, and his deft henchmen
Riffle the tabloids—that keeps us.

Over the campfire the desert moon
Slivers the west, too chaste and cleanly
To mean hard luck. The man rattles the skillet
To take the raw edge off the silence;
The woman lifts up her heart; the Infant
Knuckles the generous breast, and feeds.

THE MAKING OF THE CROSS

Rough fir, hauled from the hills. And the tree it had been,
Lithe-limbed, wherein the wren had nested,
Whereon the red hawk and the grey
Rested from flight, and the raw-head vulture
Shouldered to his feed—that tree went over
Bladed down with a double-bitted axe; was snaked with winches;
The wedge split it; hewn with the adze
It lay to season toward its use.

So too with the nails: milleniums under the earth,
Pure ore; chunked out with picks; the nail-shape
Struck in the pelt-lunged forge; tonged to a cask,
And the wait against that work.

Even the thorn-bush flourished from afar,
As do the flourishing generations of its kind,
Filling the shallow soil no one wants.
Wind-sown, it cuts the cattle and the wild horse;
It tears the cloth of man, and hurts his hand.

Just as in life the good things of the earth
Are patiently assembled: some from here, some from there;
Wine from the hill and wheat from the valley;
Rain that comes blue-bellied out of the sopping sea;
Snow that keeps its drift on the gooseberry ridge,
Will melt with May, go down, take the egg of the salmon,
Serve the traffic of otters and fishes,
Be ditched to orchards . . .

So too are gathered up the possibles of evil.

And when the Cross was joined, quartered,
As is the earth; spoked, as is the Universal Wheel—
Those radials that led all unregenerate act
Inward to innocence—it met the thorn-wove Crown;

32

It found the Scourges and the Dice;
The Nail was given and the reed-lifted Sponge;
The Curse caught forward out of the heart corrupt;
The excoriate Foul, stoned with the thunder and the hail—
All these made up that miscellaneous wrath
And were assumed.

The evil and the wastage and the woe,
As if the earth's old cyst, back down the slough
To Adam's sin-burnt calcinated bones,
Rushed out of time and clotted on the Cross.

Off there the cougar
Coughed in passion when the sun went out; the rattler
Filmed his glinty eye, and found his hole.

GETHSEMANI

I

Seed of the earth
Rain-loosened: foxtail, filaree;
Seed of the wild grass new-bladed,
Broken from winter,
Drenched with the dew of nightfall,
Hemming the grove of olives;

Which, its each tree a black
Earth-hugging clump,
Deploys downslope,
Creates the scene's dim format.

Behind, the abandoned farmhouse,
Whose starved-out owner
Broods in the distant slums,
Sinks in the noiselessness of all neglect.

The broken harrow rusts by the barn,
Where the hireling
Turned his indifferent hand.

Above, the windmill
Screws out its iron whimper,
Voice of the veering year.

All, all in the souse of the paschal moon.

How soft, how still,
Lambent, the outlying fields,
How open, under this little height,
Rife with the surcharge of spring,
How rich—and the raw
Smell of the plough.
These are the nights a man and a woman
Wander the orchard,

34

Drunk with the odor of plum-flower.

Far off, a new lamb, restive,
Bleats in the hush;
Dark in their hutch
The barnfowl shift and jostle.
The big rooster, whose fate it is
To try this night the thin
Fidelity of man,
Sleeps on, his harsh cry
Kept near his craw.

Out there, as ever,
Night upon night,
The city, sleeved in the haze of fires,
Stains the sky.

II

Whatever the flesh may suffer
The soul suffers before.
After the feast's exultance
The Master, made pensive,
To the deserted grove
Withdraws. The Chosen, who keep
Every anxiety, about Him move,
Questioning. He turns aside;
The brow clouds over; the eyes
Even more gentle now
As pain proves in them.
They see him kneel; the festive joy
Freezes in their bones.
They see him shudder, raise
The outlifted arms, cry up,
Pitch forward,
Fall . . .

Is this the Savior of the World
Who, on His knees,
Sucks in the hurtful breath
And faints with fear?
Flesh can fear,
Soul can fear affliction,
And Christ feared both.
Power had proved his Godhead:
Miracles, a fast
Lightning track of divinization
Blazed across Palestine.
But that the God was man,
That the man could faint,
This the world must know.
And the knees give;
Time's enormous woe
Settles and spills,
As in the fire-tempering night
The mountain shakes on an ancient suture,
Sinks its stone.

Somewhere the nails
Sift rustflakes in their hoop-bound keg.
The cat-o'-nine-tails
Droops on the bailiff's wall.
But now the sullener burden
Settles on that brow.
The greater scourge,
Grasped already in the future's
Thong-wrapped hand,
Will fall, will fall forever
On the flesh of man.
The great ominous Flogger,
Off in time,
Hunches his hairy shoulder,
Waits.

The loaded whipbutt
Taps on the knobbed hand.

Whatever the world will suffer
Is here foresuffered now,
Facedown on the plough-tossed earth.
The heart, pregnant with man's eventual woe
Unpents its groan.
Here Stephen turns the innocent
Unquestioning face
Into the outflung stone.
Good Peter, upside down,
Straddles the Roman sun,
His legs like aquaducts
Bloody the down-hung head.
Already here the packed arena fills;
Its martyrs mount their yardarms.
The starveling lion
Snuffs the blood-stung air,
And the maiden's coif
Mats the tiger's jaw.
All, all are here. Their pain
Reaches already to this swollen Heart
That lugs and labors like a giant sea
Clasping its wounded islands,
Toning its solemn note upon that shore,
To weep out its geologic woe alone.

Is this the dream that God must dream in man?
The uncheckable sinners,
Who never will be warned,
Falter, look back,
Step out the determining step,
Stumble and go down.
As do those dark-delighting bats
That nightlong flitter on the bullrush sloughs,
And at the wisp of dawn convene,

Circle reluctantly,
Touched by the ravelling light,
Till daylight drives them,
The plaintive-twittering flock,
Into the gulfing cave.
So do the damned, those Light-deniers,
Indriven on their choice,
Wheel raggedly,
Caught in the terrible downdraft,
Flutter in panic,
Are sucked in.
Here at the instant of decision
His scopeless love enfolds,
Wraps them in tenderness,
Pleads.
They break away.
The vast Heart bleeds.
Hell's orifice eats them all.

Miserable generations!
When will they have a stay?
Time, the durance of finite being,
Darkens their passion-shrivelled hearts,
Breaks their knees.
They go.
All the devices of sin's deforming hand
Heap on His flat-pressed flesh.
He takes them. Each century
Explores its own avenue
To degradation. Each century
Fondles its own indulgence
In the lassitude of self.

Nor ever has a stay.
The Mystical Body,
Slit with each instant sin,
Suffers their comprehensive loss,

Bleeds forever on the man-constructed,
Man-supported Cross.

The Godly grandeur
Webbed of the human mien.

Such is that Chalice
Even the inclusive Mind
Flinches to assume;
The mereness of the man,
Though not the greatness of the God,
Falters to feel.
A total future's bodily test of faith
Crushes with consequence,
Poises, and the brow
Brightens of sweat, of blood;
The hurt mouth breaks; the eyes
Turn back to know
How men meet with their hour,
Keep God's solitary troth
And help redeem their fall,
Only to find
The best of humankind
Snore by the wall.

The city simmers its fires,
Stains the sky.

What hope from it,
Sunk in its purblind role?
What hope for it,
Drunken in slumber?
The sleep-filled faces,
The thousand-thickened dreams?
Slack mouths slobber the pillow,
The tilting heads
Nod together;

Light hands that loosely curl,
Light arms that cross.
Careless the updrawn knee,
The cotton-swaddled loin;
Careless the man
Near to the woman lain,
The dreaming child beside.

The rooster,
Sunk in his ruff,
Unconscious,
Twitches his stringy throat,
Waits for his fatal cry.

One hour.
Two.
Nor ever would be
Night longer.
History's prodigious sum
Is tallied in its onrush,
Its grim arithmetical meaning
Caught on this night's black decimal,
Turned.

History is always wrong.

The city's childish dream,
Smoky with sullen cravings,
Stains the sky.

Which of the nameless hordes
Is worthy to bring the burden on?
Which of the indigenous kingdoms
Will rise,
Fullfill the preach of prophecy,
Assume the fateful risk?

All in the wrap of dream,
All in the rush of wish.

The city
Steams in its sludge.
Is that Jerusalem,
Soughing the muted nightvoice of all towns?

Far off the herdsman
Marks the rescinding hour,
Chunks up his dungfire,
Dreams.

The Godly grandeur
Groans of the human mien.

III

What was the worth,
Back there, of that attempt,
Back at the pristine start
When all was innocence?
What was the worth of that attempt
That gave the vast Undoing its clear chance?
What was the gamble's worth to God
That He should risk the try to such as those
Who threw the gift away,
Brought mankind low,
And loosed such sordidness
The all-loving Son
Himself must take the mortal frame,
Bide out the thirty and three,
Clutch at the pain-stitched side;
And the Mystical Body
Suffer its centuries,
Riddled by human strife,

Soiled by human sin,
While such as you and I
Snore out our fitful hour
There by the wall,
And let the future fall?

The city stains.
Jerusalem.
Rome, half dead,
Stinks with its crime.
Athens lips its dust.
The luminous face of Paris
And London's puckered brow
Match looks in time;
While brash New York
Fingers its blithe heart.
Stains . . .

Sleepers
Stir by the wall
Where last year's wild seed
Took refuge from the plough.

The slumber-clammy mouths
Taste their bitter tongues,
Swallow and dream on.

The rooster, his muscle
Stiffening on the rail,
Thrashes his saw-tooth comb,
Skins his eye.

O terrible brood of the wasted fallen years!
Footloose loungers in Paradise!
You sunburned nudists under the fig-trees of Eden!
Would you have stayed your hand
Had you but seen your son

Shoulder this hour?
Would you have left the apple
Redden on the bough,
Go ripe,
Snap in the tightening cold,
Drive to the dust,
For autumn's bright
Inconsequential windfall?

Would you have left it lie
Until the small-boned deer
Dainty among the frost
Came down by night
Out of the redwood canyons—
For them, wholly a harmlessness,
But not alas, for you,
No, not for you!—
Came down by dark
To crunch its toughening rind,
And still to leave the unbitten half
Day by over-covering day,
For the yellow-jacket's winter-pestered horde
To suck all sweetness out,
Until the first rains found it where it lay,
A rotten cider-smelling husk,
The slight cost of Innocence,
Surely small price to pay
For Immortality!

Mother of men!
Dear culpable darling of our breed!
If you could see His visage in this hour,
Drenched, its whole perfection
Seamed across with pain's malignant touch,
And tomorrow's degradation
Written on that brow—

No! No! We may not ask!
That question may not be!
Not yours to say;
Not yours, nor is it ours,
Wholly to see—
But only to obey!

There did it turn,
Small, crabbed,
The least fruit in Eden,
But all the knowledge and all the woe
Clasped at its core;
It turned,
It turned on the bough.

One, only, among us
Would not have made that reach.
She on this night alone is not asleep.
But in the shut seclusion of her cell
Kneels out the rivering hours.
And where, soon now, the crucifix
Will write its graphic intersection on the wall
There has she set her gaze;
And on her anguish-written face the tears,
As on His knotted one the sweat;
And on her bitten lip
The outcaught sigh,
As on His blooded one
The sharp unanswering cry.

Christians far hence,
Engrossed in the stark account,
Will mark the outcry and half-doubt—
As if the Godliness might here be proved
Less than the fact asserts.
But what is the cost of choice?
Who may truly name it?

44

There had to be a reckoning made
Commensurate with the crime,
An act of unforgettable fitness,
For which no lesser deed
Might ever be shown to answer,
For which no greater one
Might ever be proposed.
This is that point in time
Where sin is seized up out of its utter shapelessness
And grappled into the heart,
A great shuddering embrace of absolute assent.

Everything else has vanished:
The reserves of courage,
The manly rectitude
And the sensitive response,
The sublime instinct for the deft
And the lovely—all that matchless
Concatenation of impulse and restraint
The perfect consciousness of Christ
So beautifully embodied—
Where is it now,
In the night, the nexus,
When darkness chokes on darkness
And only agony endures?
Broken,
Struck down,
Wrenched asunder,
Torn from the fragile synthesis,
To leave it mutilate.
Where all was perfectness and peace
Reigns now the corporate rancor
Of an unregenerate race.
The hours of Gethsemani
Tread out their brute reduction,
Until is left at last,
Isolate,

Like a kind oflight,
The absolute
Essentiality of what impels there.
And nothing more.

This is Love.
The final thread, the ecstasy
No suffering could break.
A love from God to God to God,
And thence to man;
Serene diamond ray
All the Passion's outrage
Could only deepen;
Nothing could scar nor smutch it;
In the proving crucible
Nothing could make it less.
There was indeed an angel,
That the future man might know
At the asking up of prayer
An angel hovers and pulls near.
(In man's abject desertion
Angels must answer!)
And yet one dares to feel
In the terrible then-and-there
Even an angel's answer
Was unpreferred
To the simple human cheer.

But that was not to be.
Hillward we slept.
In the earth beneath our head
The gopher shuddered
And drilled on, impervious.
Let the fist be knuckled,
Let mobs make hubbub,
And in the listening hills
The desert foxes

Lift their brigand-visage muzzles
To a sun-blacked sky.
The choice, here taken,
May not, here after,
Ever be denied.
All has been earned,
And earned, needs but be emptied,
A work which waits on time,
And time may run at will
That here, spent of the malefic incidence
To block, deny the day,
Wastens all fury on the utter flesh;
The future is secure.

The rooster
Stiffens his hackle,
Claws the gummy rail.
Down near his blind bird heart
Readies that terrible cry.

Fresh wind, the valley's
Long conditioner,
Freed from the haft of midnight,
Already drums the rhythm of the dawn.
Far down its length,
Light-tipped with buds,
It quicks and dartles,
Stirs on the checks of vineyards,
Where vine
Reaches to vine,
Each twisted on its stake.

Ash at the vineyard's edge,
Grey ash of the burnt
Prunings of the year,
Pocked with the dent of rain.

And when upon our brows,
Each year,
The immortal Ash
Marks us for God;
May that mark,
Struck on the declarative face,
The written Sign
Of this night's grim
Agonization,
Purge us,
Make us a fit
Habitat
For the Bread
And for the Wine;
Renew us in the eternal Covenant
Launched outward in His members
On His earthly quest.
Through Him,
Mankind broke out of History,
Who waited in the Virgin's womb
The nine ages of His knowledgeable gestation,
And walked on flaming feet,
And wrote the mark of liberation
Everywhere on the wondering human face.
Let the ignorant rooster
Riddle every sunrise with his cry.
No more have fear.
Advent is past.
Epiphany, its blazing
Declaration done.
The long Lent closes.
Before a new day drops
Man's terrible penance
Will be lifted from his back.

And now the night alarms.

Far off the posse
Gathers its torches up,
Unfolds
Its sullen plan.

Good Friday
Draws like a scalpel
On the mordant
Soul of man.

THE MASSACRE OF THE HOLY INNOCENTS

It was well in the season of the midwinter rains
But they had withheld; and in consequence
The land lay naked under a frost:
Day sky filled with a frozen light
Weakly out of the south,
And the night sky quick with stars;
So that we rode, that morning,
In the sharp hours before sun-up,
Well-buttoned; and the raw air,
Rare with frost, bit hard at our faces.
We took the way through the vineyards,
And in the first of the light
Saw that the vines were mostly unpruned,
Matted under the summer canes,
Each huddling its stake;
But some of the vineyards were half-pruned,
The one part rough with the thick
Disorder of natural growth, the other part
Neat and tidy with human care;
And somehow this was a consolation.
All the valley lay stretched and whitened about us
Under the tenseness of frost,
And the shaggy-backed farm dogs
Bayed our passage along the road.
At sun-up we came to the miserable place
We knew for our destination,
And there deployed, variously, in squads,
Some to go here, some there,
Among the mean dwellings of the place;
And among the dwellings that bordered the place;
And from these dwellings
Removed that which we came to secure;
And in the little plaza,

Before the eyes of the inhabitants,
We did what we were sent there to do,
So they might thenceforth remember that kingships
Are not sprouted like mushrooms, overnight,
From the backyards of villages.

For that was the day we were sent out to kill a King.
We thought it a joke.
Among those hovels, those inhabitants,
It seemed a joke. But when it was done
It seemed no longer a joke. Something there was,
Under the swordblades, unspeakable;
Some surging qualification,
That stung out of the spilt blood,
And swept through the welter of circumstance
Where we stooped and butchered.
How many centuries of forgiveness
Burst out of the hems of the split tunics?
How many decades of prayers were to go up to God
For the murderous hand that was not ever held?
Wherever we walked thereafter History marked us.
No matter where we drowsed, scratching our sleeves
In the tawny light of September;
No matter what water we drank of,
Watching the leaf offshore in the plucking eddy;
No matter what dreams of grandeur
Ennobled our sleep on the straw ticks of our barracks,
History stood by our side and said: these are the ones.
We died, for the most, years later,
Scattered, in other legions, under other swordblades;
And in the aftermath of death we found our clarification,
Which is a terrible thing, to know how *wrong* you have been,
And remains the strictest part of the torture.

We rode back, that day, with the sun
Moved into the south, and everywhere
The vine-dressers were well at work,

To gather the prunings up of the vines
To be burnt. The tall columns of smoke
Ascended about us into the subdued
Magnificence of the winter sky.

THE FALLING OF THE GRAIN

Amen, amen I say to you
Unless the grain of wheat falling into the ground
Die, itself remaineth alone.
But if it die, it bringeth forth much fruit.

—ST. JOHN'S GOSPEL

I. TOWARD SOLSTICE

Wrapped to the branch the runner
Rings its yearly span.
Man is made for the woman.
And woman for the man.

Stalk of the weed is stiffened,
And stands, and will be dried.
But the Word of God is prior;
It may not be denied.

The summer burns and blazes,
The year begins its drouth.
I watch the one I nevermore
May kiss upon the mouth.

II. THE PORTENT

The black king fell.
"Sorrow for the king." The black queen
Fell beside. "Sorrow for the King
And Queen," you said, "but love—"
For the red heart rose. "Sorrow
For the King and Queen, but love . . ."

We read the cards for sport,
But how press back the tears at such an incantation?
You, in the prescience of the truly fated—
That was the thing in your voice, then,
When it rang in the room,
And sorrow and peace were at one in your face,
And you knew my grief,
Which was indeed joy.

"But love, but love—
Sorrow for the King and Queen,
But love . . ."

Most beautiful, wholly tender and true,
Sad prophetess, weep indeed in the soul,
But the smile redeems.

I shall forget many nights but never that.
The moon was cut. The last train
Rested on its ramp, and all the bridges home
Were empty of their fare.
The next day was the Lord's. Beyond it
Rose the immitigable week of His great word,
Schismatic in our lives.

III. THE QUITTANCE OF THE WOUND

But God is good. Nor has ever, once,
In His keeping of this world,
Worked an evil in men's lives;
Not in all those losses, those takings,
The dark denials each in his time assumes and must ponder;
Nor in the great deprivations exacted of His saints,

When He would seem to have broken them in His bare hand
With His love and His wisdom—
Not once has He ever
Wrought an evil in men's lives.

Only the flawed of heart foul Him.
Only the blind, a fist pitched at the sky,
A mouth smoky with imprecation;
Or that sullen hutch of the heart's embittered brood,
Like the serpent's egg
Hatched out in the breast.

But as for these, His own,
These, who served as His saints,
These, in the luminous purity of their love,
Knelt down on their deprivation,
Dipping the very wounds of self
In the painful balm of that compliance;
And let that piercing Finger
Probe to an inmost hurt,
Nor shrank to be traced.

These have taken the plight a trust entails,
And not doubted, and have counted
Every tremor of the soul,
And that long cry of woe
Shut back down into the cropped heart,
As only the cleanliest quittance
Against the rapture of His face.

And have put forth a hand to take up the loss,
Though fear be with it.
And the hand sustains.

IV. THE CROWNING OF THE QUEEN

So that you, too, whom I have loved,
Who have worn my name as wife,
Which was my pride in your wearing;
And I beside you, on these streets, knowing myself
King indeed with such a queen—
You now have laid aside that queenship of the king
To take another kind of crown;
And I see how purity,
Assumed into the unrancorous heart,
Has lifted from your face a sorrow's cleft,
And made you radiant—a love
Greater than ever yours or mine,
Who in our humanity
Could but work through these meshes
Toward that wide comprehension
Where God keeps His own
In the grandeur of His own.

So do you now
Move through my mind,
And in your queenliness
Are still supreme,
Who have that gentleness
The deeply hurt but purely healed
Bring back to the world.

V. IN THE RIPENESS OF THE WEED

And now it is summer.
And the strong weed
Shoulders the fence,
And the weak weed
Scatters,
And all things
Hold increase.

And the summer
Burns, and I remember mornings
Risen one from another,
But must put aside that thought now,
Save maybe in rising
To note but the single
Print in the bed.

But there is a greater
Glory that one may come to,
Whence even that other
Gets its flame.

This we take.

Therefore do I salute that magic of yours
This last time in my poems, my wife—
We who clasped in the high try at holiness
Where holiness never could be;
And are now, since we must, at last content,
To seek where it more purely is.

And the strong weed
Seeds, and the weak weed
Scatters, and I see in them each
A glory of God;
And am made grateful,
That of His help
Can put down now the pride of the flesh
(Which had not, heretofore, been my ability)
And am humbled,
And not given to rankling
(As I was)
When the ripe weed
Seeds, and the weak weed
Scatters.

Now it may happen that one
Who is himself a binder of books,
Sometimes, too rough with the needle,
May pierce to his hand, and by chance from that pierce
Let fall his blood in the book;
Then does he, seeing it,
Cast out that leaf as blemished,
Because there is blood on it.

But in the book I bind for you
Rather do I now take up that leaf
And bind it in. For as our blood
On the leaf of this life is surely no blemish to God,
So do I trust that my blood in this book
Will be no blemish to you.

For it is by blood that we are made dear.

It is by the blood of Our Lord each day in the Mass
That we are perfectly endeared to God;
And therefore will it be by the mingling
Of His blood with ours on the smutched page
Of our life, that we may hope to see endeared
The smutched page of mankind in that otherwise
Blemishless book of His Works.

And as my blood is alone on the leaf,
So on the leaf of this life
Must it also remain alone from yours.
Yet do I pray that in the broader Book
May these mingle, and be altogether
Quenched in that brighter Blood,

Which burns, and is the true
Letter of life,
And pure on the page
Makes up the rare
Rubrication of the Word.

VII. PAST SOLSTICE

Past solstice: not yet the length of a month past;
And now to leave, to go forth from the house,
Aware of a first lack in the light
Where the excesses of light had sprouted.

So. That autumn edges? Days go short?
Is it not of God's hand, all?

As in the North, remember, at the year's
Change again toward its final quarter,
After the somnolent summer held sustained its peace on the sea,
And threw a different face on the sea;
Then would the autumnal gales be blown in at night,
And we saw how the inswell of storm,
That had troubled the face of the water far out,
Disturbing those listless nooks of the tide,
Those eddies, where all stagnant summer the sea held to its hoard,
And now brought forward: shells, bottles, glass balls, pieces of wreck,
Many wonderful shapes, many wonderful things of the drift,
Strewn flotsam gifts of the ocean-going fleets,
All there, all to be touched—but at next tide
As solemnly gone, quite taken,
That glittering beach
Far as the sight fell,
Picked clean. Even the gulls
Gone.

And yet the sea was the same;
The Sea was the source in which all tides were manifest.
It was the Sea we went to.

So God in His seasons.
And the God-seeker, the man God-loving,
He will not worship entire
Opulent Fall, nor sparse Winter,
And will let frolicsome Spring
Go its own way for once.
But will look rather to that eternity *within* the flux,
Where the source of all seasons
Holds them back at His mighty Heart,
And breathes on them in their order.

For the seasons seen are only the things of time,
And time seen is only the order of things,
And all things will fail.
But the Source of all things will never fail.
For the nature of things lies in their being apart,
They may suffer reduction;
But the Source of things is not fashioned of parts,
And may not be reduced.

And we, being things, love things, and the sequence of things.
We love the seasons. But what we seek of the thing
Is that greaterness within the thing
Which keeps it in being.

Therefore praise Autumn, praise opulent Autumn,
And breathe the white breath of Winter,
And revel with Spring.

But love what Autumn
Will never succeed,
Nor Winter curb, nor Spring survive;

What even Summer, the tall
Triumphant Summer,
Will never surpass:

Love Him.

VIII. ADVENT

Fertile and rank and rich the coastal rains
Walked on the stiffened weeds and made them bend;
And stunned November chokes the cottonwood creeks
For Autumn's end.

And the hour of advent draws on the small-eyed seeds
That spilled in the pentecostal drought from the fallen cup;
Swept in the riddled summer-shrunken earth;
Now the eyes look up.

Faintly they glint, they glimmer, they try to see;
They pick at the crust; they touch at the wasted rind.
Winter will pinch them back but now they know,
And will not stay blind.

And all creation will gather its glory up
Out of the clouded winter-frigid womb;
And the sudden Eye will swell with the gift of sight,
And split the tomb.

THE SCREED OF THE FLESH

Be not as the horse and mule,
that have no understanding.

—PSALM XXXI

I cried out to the Lord
That the Lord might open the wall of my heart
And show me the thing I am.

All of my life I walked in the world
But I had not understanding.

All of my life I gloried self,
Singing the glory of myself;
I let the exuberance of the self, the passion of self,
Serve for my full sufficiency.

But all of my life I knew not what I was:
The thing I was, it had not understanding.
It ran like the colt in the field,
That takes its delight in the pluck-up of its foot,
In the looseness of its mane;
That takes its pleasure in the lift of knee,
The liquid action of the knee;
And has no end except its running as its end,
Nor asks of what it runs, nor where;
But runs, and takes its glory
In the swiftness of its run.

So I. I took my glory
In the running of the heart,
Knowing it good;

And darkled my days with ignorance.

I darkled the fields of my childhood,
The country roads of my young manhood,
And the streets, the streets of my full maturity.
All these, the darkling days of my ignorance.
And did run, and reveled in the run.
And knew not where I ran, nor why,
Nor toward what thing I ran.

I ran, but I had not understanding.

As the greyhound runs, as the jackrabbit runs in the jimson;
As the kestrel flies, as the swamphawk flies on the tules;
As the falcon stoops in the dawn, as the owl strikes in the dusk;
I flew, but I never knew the face of the Light that I flew in.

Lord, Lord, as the coupling horse, as the bull and the ram,
Who cover, and who dispel themselves in the creature of their kind,
And fall back, and the seed of their kind is left in the creature of their
    kind,
But they know it not: the waste of the seed of the self
Stains in the shaggy hide, and they know it not.
I stood in the stain of my own seed and had not understanding.
I lay in the coals of my burning, and knew but that I was burnt.
I had not understanding.

And when I stooped to drink at the cistern could not but quench my
    thirst.
Nor when I ate of the pomegranate, nor when I tasted of the grape,
(The muscat or the sultana, the malaga or the black);
When I crushed in my mouth the fat of their mast,
Could not, could not but eat. Ate only. I had not understanding.
Nor gave I thanks, nor the thought of thanks,
Nor spoke up, ever, my debt of thanks, as each day
I was endebted, as each day I could only be
By the free spilth of Thy giving.

Lord, Lord, I ate, but I had not understanding.

*

For how shall the eater who eats but the passable thing of the earth
Be filled with his act of eating?
Belly will fill; blood will fill of the eaten thing; body will fill.
Bowels will fill of the eaten thing; dung be given back to the earth
That the eatable thing might be.
Earth consumes and sea consumes and the element of air consumes;
So shall the perishing things of the self return to the things they are.

For what did I hope of this thing of self that I sought to give it glory?
Did I think this lovely thing the flesh is more than of dung that is
    dropped?
Did I think the flight of the hastening foot, the lilt in it, the leap that is
    there;
Did I think the beautiful breathing of runners is more than the stain
    of their sweat?

For the earth assumes these things of its own, taking them back.
It takes up the things of which it is made, it forever recovers.
Sea recovers, air recovers the spending breath of runners.
Each recovers its own; each receives it back.
The beauty of running men and of beasts, the gleam of the horse and
    the whippet;
The music of woman in motion, that wink of the heel and the arm,
The waist that is supple and drawn—O glory of earth
In the pulse of the carrying knee! O, glory of God-created earth
In the pace of the fabled ankles!

These are the things we have as the earth, as the shimmer of earth has
    our love.
And these the earth recovers, for these are the things of its own.
All these does the earth recover, the earth and the air and the sea; each
    assumes them back;

64

Almost as if they were never meant to be more than the thing they
        were made of,
Nothing more than earth, than air, nor anything more than sea.
As if the earth begrudged them, and badly wanted them back.
As the earth wants back the ash of the grass in the smoking fields of
        October,
When the sun-struck face of the hill is burnt to make for the pastures
        of spring;
As the earth wants back the black on the rocks when the hill is burnt
        for pasture.
There the bull's head falls on the stubble, the bone of the bull is
        tossed;
The sheep's head gleams on the hill where the skulking cougar
        dropped it;
The bones lie white and scattered, the slotted hooves lie thrown.

(And the dawn coyotes
Snuff them, and pass
Over them, and are gone.
They go like smoke in the thickets.
The hunger of beasts
Snuffs dried bone on the hill;
For the hunger of beasts
Is filled with the flesh of beasts,
But the flesh of the beast will fade.
The hunger of beasts will find no filling
When the flesh of the beast is gone.)

I lay on the hill as a beast of the hill which I knew as the hill beast
        knows.
I sang as the linnet, that sings from a throbbing pride of self
Just to be singing. I sang as a bird, that bursts with a bigness of heart,
And makes it to sing, nor ever asks of the source of its song,
But sings for the singing. I sang on the steepness of the hill
Nor knew why I sang.

Lord, Lord, I sang, but I had not understanding.

Lord, Lord, I sang, but the mouth of my soul was shut.

                    *

The mouth of my soul was utterly stopped with the wadded rag of my
    self,
As the truthful man who would speak of truth is gagged and kept from
    speaking;
As the mouth of a man of terrible truths is stuffed with a wad of rags,
So I gagged my soul with the stuff of self, I gagged it and led it away.
I took it down to the cellars of self where the ear of the mind is deaf;
To the clay and earthy walls of my pride where the sewer sucked in the
    dark;
Where the gross spore lurked on the table and the lewd spore throve
    underfoot;
Where the rat-wad dried on the dish and the mouse-print slept in the
    dust;
Where the things of the self were wholly contained in the world of its
    own creation,
There did I gag the truthful voice that it might not ever be heard.

I had a savior in my soul
But I riddled his brow with prickles.
I had a good redeemer
But I nailed him to a post.

And I threw his body down in the dark that the drains might drain it
    away,
That the restless sea might eat of it and the eating earth erase,
That the death air of the cellar might wholly dispel its voice.
For the earth and the air and the salt of the sea will take of their own
    and dispel it,
The things that are truly of their own, each will surely dispel.
And I gave that good redeemer up for the act of their dispelling.
But earth and air would not dispel, nor the sharp-set salt of the sea.
None of these would dispel him, on him they would not work.
For the leaching acids within the earth, they would not eat of my soul,

Nor would the salt sea stanch it, nor would the air erode.
The very iron of earth they eat, the hard gem and the agate;
But the soul that I sank in the drains of self, of this they would not eat.

But it rose from the swirling dust, it rose from the salt of the sea;
It walked on the swirling water, it stood on the sound of the sea.
And the air made room to pass it, the raw air turned aside;
The wind it would not take it, the air it let it be.

                                          It said:
O one not made of matter, on you I hold no claim!

And the earth cried out, and the sea cried, and the salts of the earth,
     they cried;
The acids that are of earth, they cried; they cried, and they would not
     eat.
I sank my soul in the salt of the sea, and the very sea disclaimed it.

And gave it back,
Casting it.
As at the recession of waters
The live thing
Lay on the edge of the sea.
And the sea lapped it,
And it lifted,
It put up its head—
As the worm,
Knocked out of the apple,
Lifts up its head,
So did it lift.

So did it lift up its own limp head
And open its own blear eye.
The soul that was given back from the sea
Looked up, to know itself not of the dead.
The soul looked up from the slime of the self
And opened its own blear eye,
Crying:

Spare Thou, O God, the thing that I am,
And give me to know my condition!

Lord, Lord, I cried in my heart
For I had not understanding.

        *

For I never had been of His knowledge, nor was I yet of His way,
Nor knew His way was the way of man, and His way the way of the
    soul.
For I saw not other than the horse or the mule, and these have not
    understanding.
I suffered but as the suffering mule, and sweat as the field horse
    sweats,
Who all day long must plod in the field, and know not why he drives,
But surely the bit will break his jaw, save but that he drives.
And the sweat of the horse makes a salt on him that dries in the
    bleaching sun,
So my sweat made stiff the garment of soul with the stiffening salt of
    the self.

And I labored, and I did lift, I trudged as the field horse trudges.
I sweated beside the sweating horse and the two sweats fell together.
And I saw there was no distinction, we were made as one in our sweat.
And I loved the horse as I loved myself, for our sweat had proved us
    one.

And I rose up from my coupling, with my seed that dried on my flesh;
And I saw the horse in his couple, and his seed, it also dried.
We poured out our sweat and our seed, and this had proved us one.
I held myself but as the horse, and was content in his lot,
To sweat in the leather and bite the bit, and turn to salt of the earth;
As the salt of my sweat fell down on the earth, with the salt of the
    earth made one;
As the salt of the horse fell down and was one with the single salt of
    the earth;

When the horse, his knees failed of driving, lay down and died on the
     earth;
That the earth and the air might have him, that the sea might assume
     him back;
So did I stop the mouth of my soul and lay it down by the horse.
For I loved the horse as I loved the earth, and the soul I would give
     back.

But the earth would not assume it, the sea would not, nor the air.

Lord, Lord, I lay my soul on the empty earth,
For I had not understanding.

       *

And what was the meaning of my soul
That was no thing of the earth?
That was no thing of the volatile air
And nothing of the sea?
For nowhere that I probed and looked
Could I find for its last place.
It was not made for this earthly earth,
It was not made for this sea.

And I cried to the Lord
That He show me the thing
That truly He meant me to be:

Made me a thing to live on earth,
But somehow not be of it.

Made me of earth and eating earth,
And somehow not be of it.

To in time lie down as the horse lies down,

But never to be of it.

Given back as the mule is given,
But never end within it.

I cried to the Lord
That the Lord might show me the thing I am—

He showed me my soul!

THE SCREED OF THE SAND

I cried out to the Lord
That the Lord might show me the thing I am,
Who showed me my heart.

O reckless with want!
Loud with the mouths of all compliance!
What did it ask for, ever, but things,
And such are the world's preference?
Nor knew to ask for, ever, but things,
And such are the world's concern?
And taking, has swept them up,
Has wept, weeps ever for more.

As does sand, stormed, upwhirled
In the withering year, when the heat-drawn summer
Makes but a dry smoke in the air,
All things of earth dead and gone dry,
Weeds of the wayside, thistle, the thorn,
All tindered up under sun,
His arrogant eye.

And out of that dryness
Does then a rising wind prevail,
And goes over the dryness;
And the dust of all things,
Whirled up, is brought forward,
So that the sandstorm
Takes vineyard, you see
The mat of its van, and it comes,
Yellow, with outlying wisps and bale forerunners;
And pre-winds enter the house,
Shutting its doors; the curtain fleers,
A flag is made of every shirt
That hangs on the line. Then does the woman
Rush forth for the bringing-in of the shirt,

And is wind-grappled, and the woman-shape
May then be seen. The vane
Gives over at last its long indecision,
But too late now
Stares in the streaming eye of the wind,
Rattling "There!" the impotent screech, the idiot answer
Everyone knows.

Such a thing
Is the savageness of the heart, a sandstorm
Sweeping the vineyard at year's change,
With the not-dried raisins spread yet by the vines,
And the whipped-over dust
Makes them be sanded.
The heart gives up to such gusts,
They blow no good, are but an ache
And an anguish, a grief
For all.

These gusts,
They are not indeed as those later
Winds of the redolent year when rains are given,
True rains of a steadier season.
These gusts are bad as those troublesome squalls
That dampen the raisins enough to botch,
And then are gone. What one awaits
Is rather the trueborn rains of November,
Floating in on their long winds,
Out of a place of a far starting,
Wombed in the girth of the sea.

And they come. That wind for days
Has known its kindlier quarter;
Watch wind breathe south for a week, content,
You know it will rain. Those rains
Come far, come deep, from a place
Eyes never have looked on,

A width and distance
No local heart ever has known,
And they bring in their wake the quencher.

They bring the nimbus, grey walkers,
The stately and slow, curling out forward,
Up from under, and darker below on their bottoms.
All afternoon they come,
Coast ranges ridden, long gone by,
Until at deep ease, at long last,
They let fall down the richnesses
Of which they are laden. The good woman
Has long since taken the shirt from the line,
Not hastily. The dust in the house
Is the house's dust, it is not the dust
Of the field. And the horse
Will put out his head through the hole in the barn
To look with his eyes, to breathe
Clean air, air with a riffle of moist for his nostrils,
Which is not the acrid air of summer;
And the horse will be glad,
For the snuff of that air means the toil is over,
And behind the horse there is hay.

Then on roofs of barns is rainwater given,
On the north of roofs, where moss
Summer-long clung dry and drab,
Is dead moss dampened: at dawn
Bright with the run-off of eaves
Moss will be vivid, a hid yellow,
Bright, lain drab in the green,
Through summer's parch,
Now is made new.

No. Not this is the squall
Of the sudden heart. (The heart
Is of sand and is sudden.)

But the true-born wind of the living Lord,
And it comes of a limitless Sea.

I cried to the Lord
That the Lord might show me the thing of my heart;
Who showed me sand.

THE SCREED OF THE FROST

I cried out to the Lord
That the Lord might show me the thing I am,
Who showed me frost.

Comes cold: those days in the bright
Youngness of the year, warm of sun,
With earth a glow, each new thing
Cut in a tingle of green:
Short grass here, long grass there,
All in the damp-set clods of winter.

Now ploughman has ploughed; the single-plough
Lately broke earth of the vineyard,
And after, the curbing plough,
Biting in close to the heel of the vine,
Cleans a sharper bite to the root
Than the straight-running mould-plough carries.
And the vine gives forth, is tender,
Each little shoot, so that the vineyardist
Keeps his team from the vineyard,
That he may not injure the shoot;
For this is the shoot to carry the grape;
This is the shoot, in the warm drift of spring,
He anxiously watches.

But wait: comes cold, and thunderheads,
Forming, let cold rain down. Hail-scurries
Rake rude toward the mountains;
Next morning at dawn the cloud lies cold,
Cold rain breaking, and a bleak wind
Crops up to clear, the raw northwest,
And in the late clear evening,
The cutting cold.

            And at dusk

The vineyardist walks in the vineyard;
He sees the young shoot. He sees
Off at the edge his plum tree in blossom,
His almond tree long past blossom;
He sees the peach trees set next his house
All in full blossom—and the shoots of the vineyard
Grown out the length of his finger,
The length of his hand. They are too far out.
Now none are not out to be spared by frost,
For a frost is coming. And the vineyardist
Walks round his vineyard. If he is given to prayer
At this time he prays; but it seems to him now
It is too late to pray. All winter long
As he loved the stove he may not have heeded,
Nor at the pruning of the vine, for it was safe;
Nor at the feeding of his chicks, for these were safe;
And mended the safe tools of the vineyard.
No thought for prayer. Winter for him
Is a safe season.

        But the spring of the year
Which is yet the fickle season of frost
Is not for him a safe season.

        And the vineyardist
Walks around his vineyard once at dusk.
At the peak of the night, too, he rises;
He looks at the quicksilver;
He walks the floor; is up with dawn.
For it is the dawn hour, the cold hour
At the seep of dawn, which is the dead
Hour of the frost.

        And he goes out.
And the dark, giving over at last,
Lets him see by the light. And he sees
How whiteness lies on his vineyard,

For the frost lies hoar and hard
Over all the vineyards. It lies white on the clod,
And makes a beard on the clod.
It lies white on the grapestake,
And makes a beard on the stake.
And all is bearded with frost.
The air is stretched with the cold of frost.
So that every clink becomes a clang.
The house of his neighbor
Shows him its whited roof,
Off there in the frost; the barn roof white,
The roofs of the outhouses, and the great heap of the tray pile,
A shoaled whale in the ocean of vines,
It too, all white. And the vineyardist
Looks to the shoot, and sees it perfectly
Held in its form, gripped of the frost, possessed
Of an unnatural beauty it could not have known
In its living greenness. For it is iced now,
And glitters, and is perfectly poised
In the magical grip of the frost.
Only as long as the frost will have it
Will it thus be held in that white perfection,
That beauty never to last.

                       And the vineyardist
Walks in the vineyard, not able to think.
The air hangs white, hangs hard. His eye
Looks off over miles of frost. His breath
Spumes out from the lip that isn't accustomed to cold,
For the mouth is breathing. Nor is there
Anything now to think: it is the long
Hour of his ruination.

                       And the veritable sun
Lets its living ray lean now on the vine.
And under that ray the first of the frost
Begins to go. And the vineyardist looks,

And sees the tip leaves curling, the tender;
They curl, but are not yet black;
They will soon be black.
And then the light mounting skyward falls on the vine
And he sees the further curling,
And a bit of the black.
And then light is up, and all is curling,
Wherever the white has been
The black will be.
Wherever his eye may look
The black will meet it;
The black and the curled,
These only will meet his eye.

Yes, the vine will live,
But not to bear.
Yes, the vine will leaf,
The leaf will grow,
But not the grape.
He must wait another year
For the grape. The grape
Is made in the early bud,
And this is the bud that is black.

Such, too, is the way the heart is.
Given over to sin,
In the fullness of sin
The heart for a time is contained.
It may find in its sin a frigid perfection
It never had known,
And holds perfection
As long as that sin may possess it—
But only until the light comes.
After the driving in of the Light
Is seen to be utterly black.

And now the vineyard blackens.

And summer comes: the vineyard
Thrives, new runners
Put forth, new leaves
Are lifted; everywhere
The luxuriant vineyard
Lifts its leaves, it thrives
In the heat of the sun.
And the stranger will stand by the vineyard,
And give it praise,
For he thinks the vineyard is rich.
But the vineyardist knows it is not rich:
There is not one grape on those vines!

I cried out to the Lord
That the Lord might show me the thing of my heart,
Who showed me frost.

BOOK TWO:
THE SAVAGERY OF LOVE
1950-1954

As that Seal upon Thy arm.

As that Sign upon Thy heart.

Thy hand

Strong as death;

Thy mouth

Hard as hell.

And the lamps of flame and fire.

—THE SONG OF SONGS

A CANTICLE TO THE WATERBIRDS

Clack your beaks you cormorants and kittiwakes,
North on those rock-croppings finger-jutted into the rough Pacific
    surge;
You migratory terns and pipers who leave but the temporal clawtrack
    written on sandbars there of your presence;
Grebes and pelicans; you comber-picking scoters and you shorelong
    gulls;
All you keepers of the coastline north of here to the Mendocino
    beaches;
All you beyond upon the cliff-face thwarting the surf at Hecate Head;
Hovering the under-surge where the cold Columbia grapples at the
    bar;
North yet to the Sound, whose islands float like a sown flurry of chips
    upon the sea;
Break wide your harsh and salt-encrusted beaks unmade for song
And say a praise up to the Lord.

And you freshwater egrets east in the flooded marshlands skirting the
    sea-level rivers, white one-legged watchers of shallows;
Broad-headed kingfishers minnow-hunting from willow stems on
    meandering valley sloughs;
You too, you herons, blue and supple-throated, stately, taking the air
    majestical in the sunflooded San Joaquin,
Grading down on your belted wings from the upper lights of sunset,
Mating over the willow clumps or where the flatwater rice fields
    shimmer;
You killdeer, high night-criers, far in the moon-suffusion sky;
Bitterns, sand-waders, all shore-walkers, all roost-keepers,
Populates of the 'dobe cliffs of the Sacramento:
Open your water-dartling beaks,
And make a praise up to the Lord.

For you hold the heart of His mighty fastnesses,
And shape the life of His indeterminate realms.
You are everywhere on the lonesome shores of His wide creation.

You keep seclusion where no man may go, giving Him praise;
Nor may a woman come to lift like your cleaving flight her clear
contralto song
To honor the spindrift gifts of His soft abundance.
You sanctify His hermitage rocks where no holy priest may kneel to
adore, nor holy nun assist;
And where His true communion-keepers are not enabled to enter.

And well may you say His praises, birds, for your ways
Are verved with the secret skills of His inclinations,
And your habits plaited and rare with the subdued elaboration of His
intricate craft;
Your days intent with the direct astuteness needful for His outwork-
ing,
And your nights alive with the dense repose of His infinite sleep.
You are His secretive charges and you serve His secretive ends,
In His clouded, mist-conditioned stations, in His murk,
Obscure in your matted nestings, immured in His limitless ranges.
He makes you penetrate through dark interstitial joinings of His
thicketed kingdoms,
And keep your concourse in the deeps of His shadowed world.

Your ways are wild but earnest, your manners grave,
Your customs carefully schooled to the note of His serious mien.
You hold the prime condition of His clean creating,
And the swift compliance with which you serve His minor means
Speaks of the constancy with which you hold Him.
For what is your high flight forever going home to your first begin-
nings,
But such a testament to your devotion?
You hold His outstretched world beneath your wings, and mount
upon His storms,
And keep your sheer wind-lidded sight upon the vast perspectives of
His mazy latitudes.

But mostly it is your way you bear existence wholly within the
context of His utter will and are untroubled.

Day upon day you do not reckon, nor scrutinize tomorrow, nor
    multiply the nightfalls with a rash concern,
But rather assume each instant as warrant sufficient of His final seal.
Wholly in Providence you spring, and when you die you look on
    death in clarity unflinched,
Go down, a clutch of feather ragged upon the brush;
Or drop on water where you briefly lived, found food,
And now yourselves made food for His deep current-keeping fish, and
    then are gone:
Is left but the pinion-feather spinning a bit on the uproil
Where lately the dorsal cut clear air.

You leave a silence. And this for you suffices, who are not of the
    ceremonials of man,
And hence are not made sad to now forgo them.
Yours is of another order of being, and wholly it compels.
But may you, birds, utterly seized in God's supremacy,
Austerely living under His austere eye—
Yet may you teach a man a necessary thing to know,
Which has to do of the strict conformity that creaturehood entails,
And constitutes the prime commitment all things share.
For God has given you the imponderable grace to *be* His verification,
Outside the mulled incertitude of our forensic choices;
That you, our lessers in the rich hegemony of Being,
May serve as testament to what a creature is,
And what creation owes.

Curlews, stilts and scissortails, beachcomber gulls,
Wave-haunters, shore-keepers, rockhead-holders, all cape-top vig-
    ilantes,
Now give God praise.
Send up the strict articulation of your throats,
And say His name.

THE ENCOUNTER

My Lord came to me in the deep of night;
The sullen dark was wounded with His name.
I was as woman made before His eyes;
My nakedness was as a secret shame.
I was a thing of flesh for His despise;
I was a nakedness before His sight.

My Lord came to me in my depth of dross;
I was as woman made and hung with shame.
His lip sucked up the marrow of my mind,
And all my body burned to bear His name.
Upon my heart He placed His pouring pain;
I hung upon Him as the albatross
Hangs on the undering gale and is sustained.

My Lord came to me and I knew, I knew.
I was a uselessness and yet He came
Shafted of the center of the sun.
I was a nakedness and was of shame;
I was a nothingness and unbegun.
The look He leaned upon me lit me through.

My Lord came to me in my own amaze;
My body burned and that was of my shame.
I who was too impure to meet His gaze
Bent beneath the impress of His name.
He broke beyond the burning and the blame,
And burned the blame to make that pain of praise.

My Lord went from me and I could not be.
I fell through altitudes of leveled light,
As, shaken into space from his mast-tree,
The lookout falls unto the patient sea,
Falling forever through Time's windless flight
To meet the waters of eternity.

A PENITENTIAL PSALM

*As eyes weakened and clouded by humors suffer pain when
the clear light beats upon them, so the soul by reason of its
impurity suffers exceedingly when the Divine Light really
shines upon it. And when the rays of this pure light really
shine upon the soul in order to expel its impurities, the soul
perceives itself to be so unclean and miserable that it seems as
if God had set Himself against it, and it itself were set against
God. The soul seeing distinctly in this bright and pure light,
though dimly, its own impurity, acknowledges its own un-
worthiness before God and all creatures.*

—ST. JOHN OF THE CROSS

Crime of my corruptness! When will it find a cease?
For look: I was conceived in iniquities,
And in sins did my mother conceive me!
Rash Eve, secretive, in the pelt of luxury engendered;
Struck forward through the mortal loins, eternal taint;
To the very soul, steeped; in stealth, stained;
With sweat, by the body's saltness, streaked.
O coarse-grained soul! O crudity! O thing of trash!
When will the all-comprehending God, offended,
Make it right? Expunge, eradicate from time?
Have but a purity of nothingness where once was I?
Not ever? Then burn! O bring a terrible breath to blow
Through every fluting of the rude worm-driven flesh!
Braise to the bone! I suffer
A day of dread in what I am! I beg
The cleanly thing I could become!

HOSPICE OF THE WORD

Maurin House, Fifth & Washington, Oakland

In the ventless room,
Over the beds at the hour of rising,
Hangs now the smother and stench of the crude flesh;
And at the grimed sink
We fill the basin of our mutual use,
Where our forty faces, rinsed daily,
Leaves each its common trace.

Is it then in this?
In this alone, then, that we find our oneness?
Who never in cleanliness, never in purity
Have ever truly met?

O my brothers! Each brings his sin-deformèd face
To the greasy pan! Is it not a terrible thing
To come upon our lives, here in each other?
In the inalienable commonality of our grosser selves?
And found there, that sign and testimonial
Of our secret hearts! Could it not have been other?
A true revealment of the soul's intent,
A freer gift, welcomed, and most dear?

Far off, in clefted rocks and dells, the springwater
Throbs out the faultless pulse of earth,
A lucent flow.

And God's sheer daylight
Pours through our shafted sky
To proffer again
The still occasion of His grace
Where we might meet each other.

But the stain remains, ubiquitous, under the thumb,
In the crease of the knuckle or about the wrist,
Or there where the lice-suck leaves its tracing along the rib.
As I, too, at night undressing, my body, its odor
Lifts like a sigh of the utter flesh:
The common breath of the poor.

"Could it not have been other?"
Moan of the scrupulous self,
Wrung outcry of the oppressed heart
Thrown back to God.

But how else and where?
Not in the urbane apartments, surely,
The suburban mansions,
Nor the luxurious hotels.

For in the crucible of revulsion
Love is made whole. St. Francis
Ran on gooseflesh toward the leper's sore;
He saw His God. Improbable and rare,
Most priceless ingredient,
It lurks behind the stubble beards;
And night after night, under the hovering breath of hundreds,
It is there; and morning after morning,
In the innominate faces soused at the shallow pan,
That in this has become like that makeshift dish
Seized up in haste without foreknowledge
That April afternoon, toward three,
When the oblique lance, upthrust,
Unloosed the floodgates of the Redemption—
How many faces, rinsed there,
Might rise, like mine, from the Bloodbath,

Almost whole? The bowl where Pilate
Damped his mincing fingers and the immortal Dish
Under the crossbeam, merge here, where the Christ-gaze
Focusses and holds. Of love, tortured and serene,
It stares from the visage of all men,
Unsanctioning, its immense pity and its terrible grief!
Or there on the nail above the sink
Where the townswoman's culled linen, smutched,
Gives back the Divine Face!
How many times each day is not that impetuous brow
Thrust into my sight, saying always:
"Not these but *this*. Look! It is I!"

O Lord and Sacrificer! I turn to meet,
But the dead sin of the inordinate self
Tentacles my heart! Take now my wrong!

And very fast, a movement
Shifting forthright through the nimbus
Of a veiled withholdance, His look
Lances, and His unbelievable mouth,
Torrent of joy, pressed home,
Shudders the rapt heart.

A JUBILEE FOR ST. PETER MARTYR

St. Peter Martyr, one of the first Dominicans, was murdered by the Cathari, a sect of the Manichean heresy, in southern Italy, in 1262. Struck down, he dipped his finger in his blood, and wrote upon the ground the words: Credo in Unum Deum.

He lived the long gestation of the Word,
That was the birth that drove him.
His death approaching out of his earliest years
Grew in him toward an ultimate emergence
His every act must verify, his whole speech affirm:
City to city the stamp of recognition
Struck on the consciousness of men.
Everywhere the luminous delineation of the Real
Swept him in the seizure of its power.
How could he rest until the truth were told
Though the Truth surpasses telling?
But there were those who knew
What a thousand vain equivocations never could contradict
One stroke of the billhook could.
Up from the bugling heart
The testament that was his total life,
But seemed to him no more than a thin
Beginning-to-be-heard, was stifled in his throat.
And the great speechlessness at last upon him,
An agony of death and deliverance grappling in his bones,
He wetted the waning finger with his blood,
And in the blindness of the dust,
As on the obdurate heart of man,
Gravened with his passion and his love,
He there set down his creed.

Springtime broke north. In backwater dells
The late-gone brant has left but the moulted pinion-feather
Sodden beside the stone, half earth already.
Deep in the hen quail's teeming orifice

The male bird's volatile faculty
Achieves its provenance; and the procreant shad
Thrusts its roe out in the siltbeds of its birth.
All things—Instinct and Idea,
The flesh-seed and the soul,
Nature and Supernature in the single grasp,
Oned in the mighty impulse—all things
Seek source. His great heart's bursting cry,
Froth-choked and gulped with air,
Floated toward Paradise,
But his soul *gleamed* there. And there his stunned sight,
That stared about him as he weakly roused,
Perceived old friendships in the hosted dead
Wreathed round in welcome; as mothers might,
Back from the birth-death darkness,
Open their eyes into the floating faces of their kin,
And have no words, only they reach, frail-handed,
Clasping and reaching, and all
Weep welcome . . .

O hosts and angels! Multitudes of joy!
Dominions and Thrones and Principalities!
God, who tempers all the angels in His gaze,
Has swept him there. The great Eye, radiant,
From out Whose scopeless orb all being pours,
Prints now His final impress on His saint.
How speak for Peter Martyr? Name his griefs?
Who now may pity him his poor cleft skull?
Back there, the immortal oath he had no strength to say,
But quickened with his passion in the dust,
Gathers behind him at the narrow Gate.
But his new eyes, opened unto Life, look only in.
Deeper than the deep star-mackerelled night
The fugal ranks of angels have drawn back,
And the fiery Seraphim no more for a moment
Pass and repass before the imponderable Face.
Gathering up his dazed divested wits,

Still half-involved in the urgence of his act,
Mute Peter tries to finish his great say.
It is not needful. But the round O of faith,
Begun back there before the billhook cropped it,
Is fashioned in his face.
As on the very instant of its birth,
Its lung as yet sealed off from the loud
Intercourse of earth, the infant
Mouths for a wail, but makes none:
So hangs his soul—

Until, merged in that last earth-parted cry,
That now, like the long articulation of his love
Arrives around him, there swells in heaven's hush
The uncontainable tumult of his joy!

THE MATE-FLIGHT OF EAGLES

A SAVAGERY OF LOVE

A Canticle for the Feast of St. Mary Magdalene, Protectress of the Dominican Order, 1952.

> *This man, if he were a prophet, would surely know who and what manner of woman this is that toucheth him.*
> —THE GOSPEL OF ST.LUKE

Spring, and the paired year:
Summer and winter clasp at the equinox.
On the slopes of Palestine
Wild mustard casts out its spilth through a surge of green.
Remote, primordial, sunken in the jungles of their superstition
The unimaginable continent dreams violently on,
Awaiting discoverers.

Earth, and the mystic enterprise;
The drama of the soul
Enacted out on the framework of the passions;
The animal nature
Contained in the thrust and seizure of its great demand.

Soul and the search,
Struck across at the level of the flesh;
The crux, twain-joined,
Two polarities athwart,
Fused at the center:
Body and soul; male and female, active and passive.
Golgotha, dead skull of the world,
Crowned above with the isolate Tree of Life.
High overhead the eagles, mating,
Circle into the sun and join there:
Four wings, one cross.

In the spring of the year the Magdalene
Crouched at the trodden foot of that Tree,
Grief-tree, tree of the desolation.
Below, the foot soldier
Shuffed his feet in the dust of the sun
And leaned on his lance.
What is this? Some streetwoman, up from the alleys,
Fallen under the falling cross,
Her garments smeared with the spittle of mobs?
No streetwoman. That flesh has burned the bed of dukes.
She hides her hands for they bleed;
None can see the wounds on her knees.
But there is plainly seen
The welt on her face where the guard struck her down.
Beautiful with the beauty of women
Disfigured in love and bereavement,
Defiant of jeers,
The fierce defiance a love is at bay.

A love savage as sin.
What has such love to do with such sin
Save that both are total, both terrible?
Crying out under the crossbeam in the totality of her love,
Whose nights went by in the fierce totality of her stain?
Forgiven much because she loved much,
Who is this, the muchness of whose love
Outmatched the muchness of her sin?
Profane mistress of men
Made in the pierce of her contrition
Bride of the very Christ?

A savagery of love.
What else may be said for it,
In its own extremity,
Bloody with excess,

The fragility of the flesh
Subservient now to a perfect demand?
Northward the Mediterranean
Sloshed all night through its sea closures,
And the saline albatross
Brought the trireme home.
Golgotha, flecked with flints,
Rooted about with scrub grasses
And the vast seeds of Israel.
The savagery of the great Christ-cry
Outcried from the cross,
Thirsting for love.
What thirst in the wounds made for love
Like the mark of the kiss
Left on the hands of lovers,
Each for each?
What is this readiment for love
But a shuddering nakedness,
The seamless robe divested,
Torn violently off,
Where the soul gazes out of its deep tranquility
And waits for the wound?

The lance lives for the wound,
The wound lives for the lance:
They are made for each other.
This is the passion engendered together.
This is the pang the Groom brings to the Bride.
This is the peace
The Bride fulfills in the Groom.

*

In the spring of the year
The Magdalene crouched at the earth-trampled cross
And kissed that blood. O chaste mouth
Defiled once by a rush of savage kisses,

What is the thirst in the chasteness of a mouth
The sudden touch of limitless grace
Has made so pure?

Over your head the Christflesh,
Whipwounded, bleeds from its total bruise.
Is your sin seen now, Magdalene?
You had no modesty in your heart,
Stripped in the exultation of the flesh.
Clothed now in a Modesty
No profane eye ever may pierce,
You too take share in the stripping of the cross;
You too take share in the fierce exposure
Between the love of God and the hatred of men.
Where is your shame but cross-nailed, O shameless,
Unshamed at last in the terrible
Nakedness of divine Purity,
You who kissed the dust from those feet,
Who wiped with the very hairs of your head
The filth of man's fall?

Magdalene! Magdalene!
Sunk like death in the clasp of shame!
What are you now in the great embrace
Where the Groom meets the Bride
In the rapture of a kiss
Perfected in such pain?

Thy shame, Magdalene!
The reckless laver of the flesh
Poured out on the cat-pelt couches!
What priceless laver
Lately poured from the broken jar,
Lavish, in the Lord's anointing,
More reckless now in the laver of your grief
Sobbed out in the sand at the terrible feet
Sagged now on the nail?

*

High overhead the sky deepens toward thunder,
It darkens and draws down.
Somber, fretted with scud,
The wisps of a reckoning storm,
It ranges in from the sea.
The cross, a gaunt finger,
The malediction of men,
Screeds the threatening sky.
To left and to right
Thieves live on,
The good and the bad,
Each judged,
But the Truth has died.

The lancer, uncertain and troubled,
Snuffing the warning wind,
Moves forward.
Under the crossbeam the streetwoman
Blazes with her intrepid face
Defiance and reproach.
But the lancer lifts the imperious lance;
And the point,
Placed to the rib,
Is pressed.
The point nudges,
It tries;
Pressed harder,
Tries.
And in the moment's pause,
The troubled lancer,
Lifting his sight,
Looks sheer in the depths of the dead eyes;
And the gaze given back
Is a gaze to the depths of his own dead soul;

And in the sudden clench of a heart convulsed,
Riven by grace,
The arm lifts;
And the lance,
Beautiful,
Clean,
A movement matchless and sublime
As the glide of a dancer,
Homes to its perfect place.

*

O indrawn lance!
O lance seated in ecstasy!
Thrust through to your long fulfillment!
How much of hunger is here assuaged in the thirst of love!
What tasting of delight where the head tastes the heart!
The flow downshaft of the blood outgushed!
What rapture at the lips of the living wound
In the seethe and pulse of the blood!
What plenitude of power in passion loosed,
When the Christ-love and the Christ-death
Find the Love-death of the Cross!
O delectation of the nails
Fast driven into the exquisite wrists,
That have brought the Christ to reach with the heart,
Endow the lance with its own love,
Thirst upward for source,
Plunge through the maidenly veils of flesh,
Till faith and love are all engulfed in the wells of desire!
O beatitude of the passion
Subdued and controlled in the channel of that grace,
When the Source-Bringer, pinned by those benedictive hands,
Reaches, in the great outreach of heart,
Making the shaft to rise, upstabbed,
Hugged in by that huge ingesting power,
Bursting through his corporeal resistances,

99

Skin and muscle, gristle and the bone,
To the final unquenchable center,
The ravished hole,
To the heart!

And beautiful as the mate-flight of eagles,
When from their wind-shuttled eyrie
They then cast forth;
And on wakening wings
Take sky;
And over the thrust
Welter and maze of wide sierra
Climb the pouring up-shaft of air;
And high where the thunderheads mushroom and coil
Turn to; and in the gyre and sweep
That is a tremendous strength of wings,
Clutch claw to claw and the beaks clash;
And in that high instantaneity
The skyborne join is made,
And all passion poured—
So is the grappling of the soul in its God.

The lance is stanched in its deep fulfillment;
All its savagery quenched of its quest.
The wound lives on like a proof.

You will go forth, Magdalene, into the dust-driven world,
Bearing everywhere about you
The stamp of a consummate chasteness;
Wearing here and there on your person,
About your hands,
Along your throat,
Across your lips,
The invisible and radiant marks
Where the Blood was borne,
The mark of the kiss the lover
Everywhere bears in the flesh as consummation.

And though the manner of your dying
May not be certified—
Jerusalem, or the Greek cities of the East,
Or, as the legend tells,
Under the sweet Provençal sky—
There could be no death you had not already died,
Its taste was your finalness,
Your rebeginning,
Of what had been begun on the day of the Death,
The day the eagles paired over Juda,
And the Cross tore a hole in the sky.

THE CROSS TORE A HOLE

A Canticle for the Feast of the Most Precious Blood, 1954.

> *There are three who give testimony in heaven:*
> *the Father, the Word, and the Holy Ghost:*
> *and these three are one.*
>
> *And there are three that give testimony on earth:*
> *the spirit, the water and the blood:*
> *and these three are one.*
> —THE FIRST EPISTLE OF ST. JOHN

The cross tore a hole.
In the spring, at the April of the year,
Among crevices of creekside rocks,
Upon the ancient earth, strewn
By the random-raking wind,
Small seeds, the winter-runnelled,
Lie hushed, lie huddled,
Inert in their dream of life.

Tall oneness.
Aloft on a naked knob,
Shut round by the sheen
Of a soon-distempered sun, the tense
Organ of rebirth
Poles up the circling sky.

Life's never-ending dream.
The common futurity of action
Merges in its shape of end,
The thing it is to make.
Lurked in the nascent form
The seed enfolds the tree,
The sperm engulfs the man.
Christ's body, flung forward
From the virgin's womb
By man's depravity,
Straightens on the straining haft,
Makes for death.
Adam's old intransigence
Fishhooks down time
To jerk the God-man on the wristed nail.
The woman itch of Eve
Is trigger to Christ's pain,
Her acrid fruit, His feast:
Retched up her poison through the slashed
Sidewinder whips.
His loins
Our life.

*

The perfect earth of Palestine
Basks in the gaze of God:
It is the season of the year.
Asphodel, shaken from the sifting
Flight of spring

Laps at the foothills like a rippling sea.
Above, sierra
Shoulders its snow.
The south wind breathes of love,
Lays down its prone
Length on the land
In the utterness of love.
Last night
Under the brow of the paschal moon
Earth lay closed in her marriage clasp
And dreamt of no such dawn.

*

Come, my beloved.

A procreant whisper of grass.
A litany of reeds
Where sluggish water rouses,
A wonderment of wind,
Its murmured word,
As it wakes, toward midnight,
Stirring in love,
In ardor bestirred.
As the beloved
Stirs in her quest of dream,
Lifting those love-beguiling eyes
On a fonder dream of life.

Come, my beloved.

And the broad grove of the orchard,
Full-budded, waiting
The strong-kneed plunderer, waiting
The kicking legs of bees,
The wanton waders,
From bud to bloom:

103

All pollen-pouring clefts.

Come, my beloved.

It is the racial memory,
Clasped embrace of seasons,
Sign of the equinox,
The language of the moon.

It is the merging of the year.

*

Tall on his masted Tree
The Lover looks on life. His smile
Replenishes the gaze of miles,
His look renews the sun.
Tall on his Tree of Life
His gritted gasp, the long
Life-going, pants its full pang,
And breathes into earth's lung.
The seedcake of his kiss
Is tongued in the Beloved's lips,
Given in the Lover's gift.

Last night
He knelt down under the gnarled tree
And offered up his love.
Last night
He lay in love-drenched grass,
Cried out the lover's agonizing cry
To leave this life.
Last night
He cramped on hard, hurt-doubled knees,
Shuddered with love by the olive tree
In the love-drench of the moon.

Jerusalem!

Under his brooding gaze
Swaying her dance of death.
Dream-sunken city,
Killer of prophets,
Fouled with red fumes.
Jezebel struts her gauds,
Shaking her ruttish flanks.
Salome kicks out her long legs.
Lot's daughters
Work their father's flesh,
Ease the low itch. Bathsheba
Cocks her tempting leg,
Yawns on her shady roof,
Primps and invites,
Bats the monarch's earth-clogged eye.
Osee's wife
Shags her lovers,
Wriggling under the loquat tree.
The dames of Solomon,
Giggling with letch,
Ply their fornicating gods,
Befoul the wise man's mind.

Dead city. City
Of the prurient dream.
Black mistress of murder,
Cringing your voluble grin of death,
You eat your own.

And the Lover looks on life.

One day,
Stooping,

Writes with his finger in the sand.
Raises his head,
Looks his beloved full in the face,
Beholds his own.

Jerusalem!

Does any man accuse thee, love?
No man, Lord.

*

Come, my beloved.

And everywhere that music,
Where the moon-mad bird,
High on the pepper tree,
The mocker,
Broke all night his tortured heart,
Broke his love-tormented song,
Tossing himself in the moon-drenched air,
The mad song of that love.

Deep down earth waits.
Her womb wakes up.
The fountain of her milk
Pulses in her blood.
Bright-breast she stirs.
Womb-wise she waits.

Come, my beloved.

It is time, time.
Has been many a year
Since the proud man cut his eye-tooth
On the bitter core.
Has been many and many a long day,

Many and many a long night,
Since we hung our harps by the waterbrooks
And wept for our beloved.
Come, it is time.
No longer now delay.
Speak with the word of thy desire.
Touch with thy sudden hand.

*

When the moon sank down
We sneaked out over the olive slope
But he never sought to flee.
We seized him in our rapine tongs,
He never feared our fists.
Mouth-struck, he kissed the hand that hit.
Man-cursed, he blessed the vilifying tongue.
We garlanded that brow with thorn.
He bowed his neck and bled.

And the day lay languid on the sill
And the Beloved roused her head.

O mystery! Deep fragrance
Of the disrobing earth
Made naked now for love.
Deep kindredness,
Now new, nor ever old.
Deep kindliness of tempered light
Laid clean on tingling tops of trees.
I have sought your meaning many a time
In foothills under sierra.
I have walked for you on river runs
Where the mallard heeds his own.
Have looked for you in stilt-flight,
Gull-guessing, shearwater swoops
At herring fests, the drawn

Dawn-dizzying trek.
Have sought for you by waterfalls
Where the pert ousel, bobbing,
Shy under freshets,
Skills her moist
Mist-ribboned nest.
Could not find out your meaning there
Made in the mystery;
Not woven of the wind alone,
Nor wave alone,
Nor drift alone of night-lain creek music,
Shuff-stoned, soft through shade,
Slupped, of the wet-worked world.
Sought so to quench all ardor up,
Shining, in shapes
Froth-forthed of earth,
Nor yet to find, shape-slack,
Left as the lover's garb is left
By the night-relinquished bed,
When the lover
Forths in the cool of the night
To taste the crisp of the moon.
So seized them, fearful,
As the Beloved,
Waking, seizes up the lover's garb
And breaks it to her breast.

I clutched to me such hems,
Creation's cowl, seized
Your rapid-running streams, clasped
The deep maternity of your hills, stretched
Prone on your plains, plunged
To your seas, wrestled
There on the roaring beach
Where the swart wave
Shot (I thought) the whole of you
Into my gap-groped arms.

I fled with your going geese,
The stooping duckhawk's gyre,
Reached where tawny eagles mate,
Beat tule-stands tumultuous,
Till the heron, startled,
Struck out with her squawking mouth,
And the indignant killdeer,
All blustering outrage,
Spun loud about my head.
All these in my madness
Seized up and hugged,
Poured passion out.
My heat of haste returning
I dropped down stunned across my couch,
Caught to my breast those empty hems
And begged for your return. I begged
Out of my whole self, my single soul,
You had not left me long.

Hush. He smiles. Is being judged
By men. Is found all worthy
Of the role. Is called up now
Before the highest court.
And none more fit than he
Of all earth's generations.
Is solemnly declared, was never
One more qualified
Among the midst of men.
On solemn oath, the conclave
Of the Church and the tribune
Of the Court. Is thus pronounced
In this great exigence.
Is not another man than he
More fit to do this thing.

And when the judgment was proclaimed
We took him, winding a great triumphal

Down through the rutty streets.
We placed his birth-right on his back, the brave
Burden of victory! Nor when he fell
Did lag, but thrust him eagerly along,
Shrilling our jubilation:
The King! The King!
And climbed the holy hill.
And placed him
Agonized upon his throne.
And held him to the sky!

Spit blood, Jew.
God damn you.
Have they knocked the teeth
Half out of your head?
Their bleeding stumps
Snaggle your busted mouth.
Stretched you out a bit
To fit that king-size cross!
Hee! Hee!
We seen yer Ma—
Little slit-tailed
Hillbilly slut
Tumbled under some
Elderberry bush—
But who's yer Pa?
Why, hadn'tcha heard?
The Holy Ghost!
Haw! Haw!
Spit blood, Jew.
Gimlet yer one good eye.
God damn you.

Come, my beloved.

And I wait at the nipples of these breasts
The sucking mouths of babes.

And I wait in the womb for small manfeet
To kick the dome of dark.
I wait for bearance—have lain long,
Have wakened and not found.
The south wind soughs in the hole of the door.
The hymen-time is dead.

                    *

The earth, hot, oppressed.
The sky filmed over, heat-holding.
Sparrows gasp in the eave-hung nests.
The rain dove broods on the roofs.

        Earthquake weather
        The old man said
        Get ready for a shake.

And the cross, hill-crested,
Ploughs with its screed-wrapped cap
The veil of sky.
Heaven's taut membrane,
Tough with a thousand
Centuries, the vinegar of man's
Inconclusive lust,
Resists the straining Nerve.

Earth shudders, her groined engrossment
Loath to take new life.
Old-whore indifferent,
Satan's sterile seed
Trickling her groin,
That dead *mons veneris*
Stabbed by a thousand
Blunt fornications—

From his tall masted Tree
The Lover looks on life.
His smile replenishes the gaze of miles,
His look renews the sun.

Tall on his Tree
The Son of Man breathes life.
His gritted gasp,
The long life-going,
Pants its full pang,
Breathes in earth's dead lung,
The seedcake of his kiss
Tongued in the Beloved's lips,
His given gift.

(Deep down earth aches.
Her womb wakes up.
Bright-breast she stirs.
Womb-wise, she waits.)

At three o'clock in the afternoon
The centuries
Groined on the ruinous spar
Lunge toward life.

Tall on its straining stalk
The seed-sack of Christ's body,
Swollen with thick
Regenerative blood,
Swells and distends.
Engulfed in sky it strains.
The hot clouds press it round.
The birth-panged earth
Hurls and uproils,
Cracks her rude mortices.
Here at the straining tip

The Nerve of God
Quicks in its ecstasy.
The forward-crowding centuries,
Eons of man's act,
Lunge and crack through.
And the fierce Christ,
Split, shaken free,
Flings up, rejoicing,
Upswung, outflung,
Larklike released,
Climbs skyward,
Hovers at the lightning's tip.
And over all the earth
Drops down the plenitudinous
Great gain, the torrential
Rains of that release.
For the great side splits.
The packed incarnate Blood
Pours to the world's black womb
The funnelling Seed.
Idea and Instinct
Fuse on the stroke of Three,
The sear and shuddering strike
That makes all be.

Storm whines.
The rent Christ-body
Flaps like an empty sack
Upon the Tree.

                    *

Thou art come.

Up from the desert,
Flowing with delights,
Thou didst lean upon Thy beloved.

In the springtime of the night
I felt in my flesh
Thy sudden hand.

Thou hast put Thy hand through the hole in the door.
My womb was moved at Thy touch.

I have entered.
Thou hast gone up into the palm tree
And taken the fruits thereof.
Thou hast made me known.

As that Seal upon Thy arm.
As that Sign upon Thy heart.
Thy hand
Strong as death;
Thy mouth
Hard as hell.
And the lamps of flames and fire.

I know Thee, God
As Thou, God, knowest Thy own.

What hast Thou done to Thy sister
In the day that she was spoken to?

My womb is awake.
Thou has breathed in my belly
And made a bourning there.

I am breached.

If I be a wall
Build on me Thy bulwark of silver.
If I be a door
Join me with Thy cedar boards.

There is no more death.

My breasts are as a tower. I am
Become in Thy presence
As one finding peace.

I am grown great.
Thou hast made a birth in me, God.
I am wombed of a wonder.

It was time and past time.

The vineyard was before Thee,
Thou hast crowded in.

I am grown good.
My perfect one
Is but one.

God knows me.
                    In me
God knows and needs nothing,
Who is.
            In Thee, God,
I am Thou.
                    O sola
Beatitude!
                My soul,
God's womb, is seeded
Of God's own.
                    My womb,
God's own, is sown
Of God's seed.
                    My soul,
Wombed of God's wonder,

Is seeded, sown.

Thou that dwellest in the Gardens
Make me hear Thy voice.

Christ-crossed I bleed.

I am One.

THE MONTH OF THE DEAD

The day is up, the sun has gained his girth,
And in the quartered sky he burns his pace.
He lets flow forward on the breathing earth
The hot refulgence of his autumn face.
But high overhead the shoreling's keening cry,
Plaintive and dispossessed, compels the ear,
Wringing the soul in the protracted sigh
Of the earth-fatefulness that shapes it here.

It is deep fall; the season hovers on;
It takes the down-curve that will freeze its breath.
One in these days cannot but muse upon
The coldness and the quietude of death;
And know a silence wakeful as the flight
Of the hushed earth into its winter night.

A CANTICLE TO THE CHRIST IN THE HOLY EUCHARIST

Written on the Feast of St. Therese of the Child Jesus, Virgin and Contemplative, 1953.

Gustate, et videte quoniam suavis est Dominus!
—PSALM XXXIII

And the many days and the many nights that I lay as one barren,
As the barren doe lies on in the laurel under the slope of Mt.
 Tamalpais,
The fallow doe in the deep madrone, in the tall grove of the redwoods,
Curling her knees on the moist earth where the spring died out of the
 mountain.
Her udder is dry. Her dugs are dry as the fallen leaves of the laurel,
Where she keeps her bed in the laurel clump on the slope of Tamal-
 pais.

Sudden as wind that breaks east out of dawn this morning you struck,
As wind that poured from the wound of dawn in the valley of my
 beginning.
Your look rang like the strident quail, like the buck that stamps in the
 thicket.
Your face was the flame. Your mouth was the rinse of wine. Your
 tongue, the torrent.

I fed on that terror as hunger is stanched on meat, the taste and the
 trembling.
In the pang of my dread you smiled and swept to my heart.
As the eagle eats so I ate, as the hawk takes flesh from his talon,
As the mountain lion clings and kills, I clung and was killed.

This kill was thy name. In the wound of my heart thy voice was the
 cling,
Like honey out of the broken rock thy name and the stroke of thy kiss.
The heart wound and the hovering kiss they looked to each other,
As the lovers gaze in their clasp, the grave embrace of love.

This name and the wound of my heart partook of each other.
They had no use but to feed, the grazing of love.
Thy name and the gaze of my heart they made one wound together.
This wound-made-one was their thought, the means of their know-
    ledge.

There is nothing known like this wound, this knowledge of love.
In what love? In which wounds, such words? In what touch? In whose
    coming?
You gazed. Like the voice of the quail. Like the buck that stamps in the
    thicket.
You gave. You found the gulf, the goal. On my tongue you were
    meek.

In my heart you were might. And thy word was the running of rain
That rinses October. And the sweetwater spring in the rock. And the
    brook in the crevice.
Thy word in my heart was the start of the buck that is sourced in the
    doe.
Thy word was the milk that will be in her dugs, the stir of new life in
    them.
You gazed. I stood barren for days, lay fallow for nights.
Thy look was the movement of life, the milk in the young breasts of
    mothers.

My mouth was the babe's. You had stamped like the buck in the
    manzanita.
My heart was dry as the dugs of the doe in the fall of the year on
    Tamalpais.
I sucked thy wound as the fawn sucks milk from the crowning breast
    of its mother.
The flow of thy voice in my shrunken heart was the cling of wild
    honey,
The honey that bled from the broken comb in the cleft of Tamalpais.

The quick of thy kiss lives on in my heart with the strike, the wound

you inflicted,
Like the print of the hind feet of the buck in the earth of Tamalpais.
You left thy look like a blaze on my heart, the sudden gash in the
  granite,
The blow that broke the honeycomb in the rock of Tamalpais.

And the blaze of the buck is left in the doe, his seal that none may have
  her.
She is bred. She takes his sign to the laurel clump, and will not be
  seen.
She will lie under laurel and never be seen. She will keep his secret.
She will guard in her womb his planted pang. She will prove her
  token.
She will hold the sign that set her trust, the seal of her communion.

I will feed thy kiss: as the doe seeks out the laurel clump and feeds her
  treasure.
I will nurse in my heart the wound you made, the gash of thy
  delivery.
I will bear that blaze in my struck soul, in my body bring it.
It keeps in me now as the sign in the doe, the new life in the mother.

For each in that wound is each, and quick is quick, and we gaze,
A look that lives unslaked in the wound that it inflicted.
My gaze and thine, thy gaze and mine, in these the troth is taken.
The double gaze and the double name in the sign of the quenchless
  wound,
The wound that throbs like wakening milk in the winter dugs of the
  doe,
Like honey out of the broken comb in the rock of Tamalpais.

Thou art gone. I will keep the wound till you show. I will wait in the
  laurel.
I know as the knowledge is of the doe where she lies on Tamalpais.
In the deep madrone. In the oak. In the tall grove of the redwoods.
Where she lies in laurel and proves the wound on the slope of Mt.
  Tamalpais.

THE SOUTH COAST

Salt creek mouths unflushed by the sea
And the long day shuts down.
Whose hand stacks rock, cairn-posted,
Churched to the folded sole of this hill,
And Whose mind conceives? Three herons
Gig their necks in the tule brake
And the prying mud hen plies.
Long down, far south to Sur, the wind lags,
Slosh-washes his slow heel,
Lays off our coast, rump of the domed
Mountain, woman-backed, bedded
Under his lee. Salt grasses here,
Fringes, twigging the crevice slips,
And the gagging cypress
Wracked away from the sea.
God *makes*. On earth, in us, most instantly,
On the very now,
His own means conceives.
How many strengths break out unchoked
Where He, Whom all declares,
Delights to make be!

ANNUL IN ME MY MANHOOD

*The Lord gives these favors far more to women than to men; I
have heard the saintly Fray Peter of Alcantara say that, and I
have observed it myself. He would say that women made much
more progress on this road than men, and gave excellent reasons
for this, which there is no point in my repeating here, all in favor
of women.*

—ST. TERESA OF AVILA

Annul in me my manhood, Lord, and make
Me woman-sexed and weak,
If by that total transformation
I might know Thee more.
What is the worth of my own sex
That the bold possessive instinct
Should but shoulder Thee aside?
What uselessness is housed in my loins,
To drive, drive, the rampant pride of life,
When what is needful is a hushed quiescence?
"The soul is feminine to God,"
And hangs on impregnation,
Fertile influxing Grace. But how achieve
The elemental lapse of that repose,
That watchful, all-abiding silence of the soul,
In which the Lover enters to His own,
Yielding Himself to her, and her alone?
How may a man assume that hiddenness of heart
Being male, all masculine and male,
Blunt with male hunger?

     Make me then
Girl-hearted, virgin-souled, woman-docile, maiden-meek;
Cancel in me the rude compulsive tide
That like an angry river surges through,
Flouts off Thy soft lip-touches, froth-blinds
The soul-gaze from its very great delight,

Outbawls the rare celestial melody.
Restless I churn. The use of sex is union,
Union alone. Here it but cleaves,
Makes man the futile ape of God, all ape
And no bride, usurps the energizing role, inverts;
And in that wrenched inversion caught
Draws off the needer from his never-ending need, diverts
The seeker from the Sought.

OUT OF THE ASH

Solstice of the dark, the absolute
Zero of the year. Praise God
Who comes for us again, our lives
Pulled to their fisted knot,
Cinched tight with cold, drawn
To the heart's constriction; our faces
Seamed like clinkers in the grate,
Hands like tongs—Praise God
That Christ, phoenix immortal,
Springs up again from solstice ash,
Drives his equatorial ray
Into our cloud, emblazons
Our stiff brow, fries
Our chill tears. Come Christ,
Most gentle and throat-pulsing Bird!
O come, sweet Child! Be gladness
In our church! Waken with anthems
Our bare rafters! O phoenix
Forever! Virgin-wombed
And burning in the dark,
Be born! Be born!

BOOK THREE:
RIVER-ROOT / A SYZYGY
1957

RIVER-ROOT / A SYZYGY

River-Root: as even under high drifts, those fierce wind-grappled cuts
    of the Rockies,
One listening will hear, far down below, the softest seepage, a new
    melt, a faint draining,
And know for certain that this is the tip, this, though the leastest
    trace,
Is indeed the uttermost inch of the River.

Or on cloud-huddled days up there shut in white denseness,
Where peaks in that blindness call back and forth each to the other,
Skim but a finger along a twig, slick off the moist,
A mere dampness the cloud has left, a vague wetness.
But still you know this too is a taking, this too can be sea,
The active element, pure inception, the residual root of the River.

Place a hand under moss, brush back a fern, turn over a stone, scoop
    out a hollow—
Is there already, the merest wet, the least moistness, and is enough—
No more than this is needful for source,
So much is a start, such too makes up the rise of the River.

Even this, even these, of little more, of nothing less,
Of each, of all, drop and by drop, the very coolness priming the wind
Alone suffices: this in itself, for all its slightness, can birth the River.

And hence such wetness gains liquid body and cups a spring,
Lipped down from a crevice, some stone-slotted vein of the mauled
    mountain,
A jet of liberation, and in so much is swiftly away.
And the spurt makes a trickle, channelling out an edge for itself,
Forming a bed of itself as it goes, a bottom of gravel.

Two join together, they find a third, the fourth sucks in making a
    fifth.
One and by one, down crick, over bar, under bush, beyond bend,

They merge and they melt, they start and they stretch.
The frozen glaciers fuse and further, the long high levels give up their
    gifts.

And now over all the rock-walls the River sweeps, he stoops and
    plunges.
He has found his scope and is on his way.
Let slopes drop slides, let ponderosas topple athwart him—
Log jams of winter, storm-sundered roots and the breakage of forests
Clog up canyons—for him these are nothing.

He has found his strength and takes no defection.
He has smelled his term in his prime beginning and will not be fended.
He carries sea in his gut: heels in the peaks but his throat at the Gulf:
Spending is all he knows.

Spending, to spend, his whole libido: to spend is his sex.

For the River is male. He is raking down ridges,
And sucks up mud from alluvial flats, far muck-bottomed valleys.
He drags cold silt a long way, a passion to bring,
Keeps reaching back for what he has left and channelling on.
All head: but nonetheless his roots are restless.
They have need of suckling, the passion to fulfill. In the glut of
    hunger
He chews down the kneecaps of mountains.

And bringing down to bring on has but one resolve: to deliver.
It is this that makes up his elemental need,
Constitutes his primal ground, the under-aching sex of the River.

For deep in his groin he carries the fore-thrusting phallos of his might
That sucks up a continent, pouring it into the sea.
A passion for elseness lurks in his root. As the father in child-getting
Draws back on his body, the furthermost nerves of his great
    physique—
Beyond the root phallos and the slumberous reservoirs of his seed,

Far up the tall spinal range of his torso, the mountainous back and the
    cloud-hung shoulders,
Above the interlinking neck to the high domed summit, the somno-
    lent skull,
Those uttermost lakes of the brimming brain—so does the river-
    phallos draw on the land.

Out of the fields and forests, out of the cornland and cottonland,
Out of the buttes and measureless prairies, out of high ridges, the
    remotest mountains,
Out of the gut, the taut belly and smouldering lava filled loins of
    the continent,
The male god draws, serpentine giant, phallic thrust and vengeance,
The sex-enduring, life-bestowing, father of waters: the River.

Flying over at dusk on a clear day, trending across it
Coiled below, a shimmer of light, sinuous, the quicksilver runner,
Deep-linking nerve of the vast continent, a sleeping snake.
You follow it down as the light fails, massive, majestic,
Thick and inert, recumbent, torpid with sentient power.

Slowly night takes it. When darkness drops on the valley
The River, iridescent, beats on through hot clay,
Its need and its passion dreaming far forward a full thousand miles:
Its head in the uterine sea.

                    For the strong long River
Leaps to the Gulf, earth-lover, broacher, dredger of female silt and
    engorger, sperm-thruster.
And behind all his maleness that mulling might.
The gnawn rockheads jut for peaks, ridgepoles of height
Where fork-lightning splices flicked roots in heaven,
Tall sap-swollen trees thrust juice at the sky,
Murmurous with pollen, their potent musk.

                         And the high cut crags.
There bighorn ram covers his ewe in a rushing tussle, the loose rock

Swirls under chipping hooves; it falls a thousand feet: when it hits
Fire flashes below.

                    And the water-delled flats.
The mountain buck springs his start in the doe,
Pine-needled earth rucked under this pitch, the rubbed antlers
        rattling.
And balsam barrens where the grizzly, sullen, roused to slow joy,
Mauls his fierce woman crazed with desire.

And lily-pad lakes where the bull moose thrashes his scoop-sweep
        head,
The huge horns flailing. In the throes of his mate-move
Tramples shallows, cattails shatter, the black testes swinging. His
        love
Dredges up sperm, souse of his juice streaking her belly,
Seed-rush to the womb.

And those everlasting plains where the buffalo bull couples his cow,
Massive, the humped mountainous shoulders, domed primordial
        hulk of his head
Reared skyward, that ponderous love.

And the randy squirrel, the scuttling rabbit,
Lolling coyote, the prancing pronghorn.

Out of the teeming maleness of earth the black River plunges.

And over his length streaked birds dip down, sip water up in their
        parching beaks,
Stagger-winged skimmers: slaked they fly on.
The beating drake, the honking gander, their necks
Arched in splendor, gabbling under the mating moon,
Knife-blade wings in that watery couple
Slashing torn reeds, a thrash of pinions. They tread down the bitten
Half-drowned heads of shy hens, a mighty thunder.
They wade through flat water.

And the fecund fish:
Great pikes in their plunge, each trailing his mate:
Quick trout dartling glib river-shallows.

                              Deep down under
The snapping turtle sulks in his cutbank hole. Over his head
Bigmouth bass break water for joy. Far back on the bayou
One bull frog swells his organ-note gong: the syllable of desire
Booms over the bog.

                    And the River runs.

                              And now at last
It rides by the somnolent night-lying cities of man,
Past pier and past factory, the long-spoked avenues hubbed on center,
Past the outlying suburbs, past wide plantations, capacious farms,
Past roof and room, the chamberment of houses, those sleep-
        bequeathing beds
Where consciousness sinks, the brain bowing at last.
It soaks up strength in slumber and in love.

                              And the man
Sleeps by the woman, husband by wife, blond by dark, their bodies
Given over now to a deepness of sleep,
But the souls adream.

                    And in that dream
Their limbs touch, the suppleness of woman
Slumbers against the straightness of man. Along her body
His own makes meaning, and out of this straightness
A trending seeks. As if, for music, to see if such a meaning is,
The murmur of sex makes a wakening within:
Deep in her dark his meaning moves.

                              And she wakens.
For there is a touch, a nudge and provocation, a slow alerting,

And in the alertness a growing tenseness.
It runs through the marrow, and out of that nerving, in ponderous
    sleep,
They roll together.

                Stark, the innominate phallos
Knocks at the door.

                And the phallos, knocking,
Finds a slow invitational yielding of entrance,
A let of approval, and is roused: his body's stem,
The root of their love, stemmed out of the male, gropes through the
    dark,
The labial embracement.

                And now they waken.

It has been between them a night this night of discontent, starving,
    and many a day.
They have flanged, split long on sheer misunderstanding, sore at the
    heart each for the other,
A soreness swollen, sick unto death, long past containment. For in
    their estrangement
Denied the flesh, their need now burgeoning, but the hearts still sore.
So once again they talked it out, finding no concord, and their
    differences
Lay like a bane, could only turn in that torment,
Each galled at the heart, edging the other.

This near midnight. Come to nothing they sank toward sleep, fitful, a
    disquieted slumber.
Outside, the great River, torpid and vast, lay dredging its dark,
That under-holding strength going south to the sea.
Over the house whorled stars hover, the apex of night peaks and goes
    west.
Under the shut moon, halved, the mockingbird
Sings all night his slow evocation.

And at last they sleep. And all the years
Inert on their lives, merging toward some total relation,
Some clasp of the twinned divisions of self, some unitive truth
No consciousness claims.

                    And strangely in sleep
The days of their childhood rise around them,
Under the forming hand of the mother, the father's
Benevolent kindness or his terrifying wrath,
Their young friendships, school chums known and perhaps forgotten,
Faces swimming the memorial void, to again emerge,
Nights under whippoorwill stars, those sundowns of dusk when all
        nature listened.
And the rare mornings, dawn streaking a sky,
The low wind crouching out of the east, its pane-blurring muzzle.

And she remembers the words of her mother,
Unspoken, woman's ancient wisdom, mystery of the moon.

And he remembers the hand of his father, powerful on the plough,
The head laved with white light.

And perhaps they dream how first they met.
A Cajun girl not turned sixteen she came out of the Mass,
Down steep church steps on a bright Sunday.
And he stood there, tall blond youth from far up the River,
Pausing outside on the sunlit pavement,
Curious, this strange Latin rite.

And they saw one another.
And so again on another Sunday,
And so again.

            And after, then, their first true meeting,
One look of utter recognition. They knew from that what each was to
        be.

Surely were they set aside, each for the other.

And he met her father, a dark man and old, of deep religion,
An earth man and a man of prayer, who looked at the sky with a look
    of knowing.
And he saw this man indeed knew God, and he feared this man.

And they married.
He stood there stiff and frowning during that Mass,
But he did stand, and he did agree to respect her religion,
And to raise the kids Catholics.

                    Nor will he ever forget
The gift that night of her hymen-gift,
Delicately, her eyes down and her lips parted.
But she raised her nightgown over her breasts
Because he turned down the covers.

                    Getting up in the dark
The mystery of woman's blood sensed on his flesh,
And all about him the musk smell, scent-drift of sex, her evocative
    presence.

And sensing that blood he thought of the Mass, and he feared.

That was the night, the fiery tingle, his blond
Blazed on her dark. She burned blue: his steel
Struck sharp the rhapsody of love,
Touslings of discovery, wonderment and delight,
Its animal rage, that love,
Sheets kicked off, her bodice broken.

In the dawn of that day she chided him, "Look, you have broken my
    bodice,"
The dark breast peeping out of the rent, and that started them again.

At the Mass he knelt, tall and aloof, puzzled.

134

The priest drank the Blood.

She left his side then and took from the priest a Bread.
He watched from his pew; he thought of her dark womanflesh in his
    clasp.
She came back from the altar, her eyes down, her lips parted.

This troubled him.

He stood up troubled to let her go by,
The myrrh of the altar faintly about her: her evocative presence.

Or later, near honeymoon's end, one hot afternoon
When between them bashfulness was no more,
She called to him softly, low-voiced,
Hardly the time of day for love, but she called him.

And going he went and found her undressed,
Half-naked in haste he took her.
They took—a savagery of splashed fire,
Kicking and clawing, hair wild, her teeth
Clicking little knives through her sobs,
Her shuddering loins, the sucked belly heaving.

And being well worn down from so much of loving, the great gantlet
    of passion,
He was long time acoming, pounding and stabbing.
And she spasmed again, then yet again, and at last he came,
The spent seed jetting out of his groin.

And they two collapsed, nor never moved again till dusk.
The summer rain, falling, plunged through the gloom,
The hot drops chafing the leaves.

Or he dreams the night of her childbirth,
And the small cry of his son.

It was this that convinced him—
No house divided against itself—
And he entered the Church: at the stone-cold font
Knelt and was shrived, baptised with his son.

And kneeling again at the altar rail
Thanked God of His greatness.
Nor was there ever a Sunday found him not at the Mass.

And he prayed.

And the second child was a girl,
And he loved that girl as he loved his life.
But his wife loved the boy.

And another girl and another boy,
The days lengthening now with incremental labor, getting food and
        fuel,
Buying meats, nights by the fire,
A prayer by the bed.

And he thought on God and prayed long on God,
And he prospered, for the land was young, and faith sustained him.

And the years swirled.
No children now for some time,
And both were content.

And they gained in wisdom.

For always the River ran by the house,
In dusk or dawn, in night or noon,
The River, running, ran through their lives.

And the mockingbird sang in the rich magnolia.

And now the night hangs swart and deep on the River.

And they touch one another, being long estranged in that human
    foible,
And the night at last giving over, past the second hour, gliding up to
    the third,
The man moving in sleep touches the woman, her slow flank,
And sensing again the slow curve, lain soft to his straightness.

And the touch alerting
He moves his hand, and their palms meet, their fingers find.
This is the time he touches her breast,
Lightly hovers the sensitive nipple, and she stirs.

And the man in his dearth, seeing at last his stoniness,
Cries out of his heart: "Forgive me!"
Crying, "I am nothing without you!"
Crying, "How wrong I have been!"

And out of sleep's finding
She buries her mouth on the arch of his throat,
And her breast burrows against him, the low curve,
Hip, flank, the mooned belly, forgiving him with her hands, her
    fingers
Groping his head, his hair in her hands,
Bringing his neck down, her fingers soothing his naped shoulders,
("My dear . . .") to slip down then to the strong fork ("My dearest
    own . . .")
Where his body trees, the strong-standing flesh ("My love . . .")
And her hands take the flesh like a thing forgiven,
And she cries out, one cry of reprieve,
Her heart opening out of her throttled pain, one ripple of joy . . .

And roused of slow fire they roll to each other and he makes an
    embrace,
The phallos knocking at the labial door, and she takes him in.

Out in the orchard, in the deep of earth,
Inch by inch the root going down gropes toward discovery,

137

Its delicate nerve probing crevices of stone, the denseness of granite,
Seeking its own way through.

And ever the River,
Its heart pulsing, the phallos
Running in the wound of earth,
The strength running seaward.

And the man in this moment, the phallos nosing within her,
Up the uterine cleft, seeking for center, the man
Feels flush that surge, stuprate, the wrestling
Need of the buck and the grizzly:
Roll her under and mount, shake the blunt phallic club,
Slog down, subjugate, make her give moan, and then
Swagger away. And in the flush of that triumph
Exult . . .

      But the blossoming need
Puts that brunt down and purely transforms it; and he, rather,
    whispering,
Murmuring his urgence of understanding, speaking to her of the
    meaning she is,
He tells her over and over what word is his truth.

And she murmurs her truth.

      And having spoken
Each to the other, and wakened within them
The one love, the one desire, the one awareness and the one com-
    prehension,
They move into concourse.

      At rest on their sides,
Torsos slightly athwart, distinct from each other,
They let themselves join. Only at the cruxed
Genital convergence, their legs lightly linked, the interlaced limbs.
So placing the twinned pelvises together, the body's weight

Falling not on the phallos; but the phallos plies free,
Easeful and free within the woman.
And she stirs on it slowly, wakening its meaning alive within her,
And then she rests.

And the man
Rests: lets all that tingling tenseness of triumph fade out of the
    phallos,
Lets it lie in her long, only the slowed breathing,
Subtly moving the clasp of her flesh on the listening phallos.
Only her bloodbeat, slowing, moving around the radiant phallos;
All their nerves, the vaginal and the phallic, ease out and relax, the
    brute
Kinetic tensions fading. And they tremble to listen.

And the blood listens.

And the phallos vibrates its throb to the woman.
The man, listening to the meaning of woman, hears her sound, for he
    is within her.
And her womb and her body, murmuring, sing the feminine mean-
    ing, and they too listen,
There in the dark, in the night bed, the world without
Swaddled in darkness.

And the great torpid River sighs south in the night.

They lie with only their sex together, they taste communion.
And over the bodies in the enveloping dark
Their four hands play, like doves that hover about their bodies.
They stroke the slow loins, they waken like wine the pendulent
    breasts.
They touch the sleek belly and softly pass on, they linger a bit where
    the pubic corona
Makes a deft nimbus, and the parts are paired.
Like doves in the dark their hands hover and play, and that meaning
    mounts.

And merging together their lips touch.

In the long kiss their souls sip oneness,
And the tongues in their mouths are entwined.

This: the whole of intentness now, this melting.
The phallos loses all life of its own, at one with the woman.
Her fire is his. In the vaginal dark
Her body has wrought its meaning of meld, he becomes that meaning.

*

And in the melding of fire
That great love gathers murmurous and strong.
They have moved in this measure out of the demarcated world,
They have touched the zone of assumed existence.
In the reciprocal pulse of a pure union
The light and dark polarities fuse,
The reconciling symbol, incarnate, joining mystery to mystery,
Annuls limitation. And in that union
Wholeness, the core of Godhead, dawns.

For God grows in them.
In the sacramental oneness
Presence flows and possesses; in the unsearchable
Deeps of that contemplation
Spirit abides; they know the wholeness of spirit.
Its mystical knowledge moves into union,
Makes a rapture within, and they worship.
They gaze in worship on the deep God-presence each wakes in the
    other,
And night contains them.

For over the bed
Spirit hovers, and in their flesh
Spirit exults, and at the tips of their fingers

An angelic rejoicing, and where the phallos
Dips in the woman, in the flow of the woman on the phallos-shaft,
The dark God listens.

For the phallos is holy
And holy is the womb: the holy phallos
In the sacred womb. And they melt.
And flowing they merge, the incarnational join
Oned with the Christ. The oneness of each
Ones them with God.

For this is the prototypal
Act of creation. Where the phallos
Kisses the womb-nerve listening
The Father is. And as the phallos flows
So is uttered the Son. And as Father and Son
Meld together, merging in love,
So here Spirit flows, between taut phallos and tremulous womb,
The male nerve and the female,
Spirit moves and is one.

How long they lie each never knows.
This prayer, their one worship. A worship
Learned in the years. For youth leans on them:
They are getters of children: known much and have suffered.
In the deeps of the soul have ached for each other,
Accepting suffering. And in the harsh acceptance
Purged themselves of the ancient hates,
The sexual cleavage. An accepted anguish
Slowly dispels the terrible fears,
The gods that govern the deep unconscious,
And emerged as true lovers.

And now in their night
They know the incarnational join: body to body,
Twain in one flesh.

And in the unitive meld
Destiny stirs. Far back in the deep seed-store of the man
Is readied the single sperm of all choice that will meet the woman.
And far down the uterine dark
Readies in turn the fated ovule made for the man.
These twain ordained for to meet this night, and so shape a soul.

This night: in this woman: from the loins of this man: creation
    gropes.
In the incarnational join of the flesh
A soul to be sealed.

Out in the night the River runs.

And now the man moves.
It is time to close: in their deep intelligence,
Thinking together through phallos and womb,
Oned in the mutual intent of arousal, they make to move.
The hands have played, have paused and enkindled.
The mouths have met, the tongues have entwined,
Every nerve-end roused and set asmoulder,
All bodily parts alert and burning.
Slow waves of incarnational fire
Flux and reflux through the joined members.
And they make to move, for seed
Must be sown that a soul might be made.

And the dark God moves them.

And the man, moving, instinctively withdraws.
Out of the dark enclosure, from the deep body returning, the phallos
    is taken.
She feels the sigh of its going, a slow relinquishment, a new expecta-
    tion.
Shifting the disposition of limbs he rolls upon her,
As out of multitudinous seas the bull whale rolling in the wave-womb
Rolls on his mate, rolls for union; and the cow whale lifts—so now the

man
Rolls to the woman, and she opens, she accepts,
She welcomes him down on the bed of her body,
Within the vale of her breasts, on the deep basin,
Between the rising encompassing thighs.

                        And the phallos is free.

Now the man, suddenly stirred, reaching down under
Lifts up the woman-weight forcefully below. And she answers,
She tenses to a bow, nerved now on a taut suppleness of support,
The torso arched from the flexed thighs, the pelvis
Verging forward and up for reengagement,
For she seeks engagement.

                        And having caught her up
Drives toward her now from deeply down under,
Sudden and strong. And she gropes the phallos
Low in her hand, and seizing it
Thrusts the blunt godhead, plunged at the labial fount,
Breathing "Now! Now!" And moving she moans.
And the phallos, oiled yet with the fragrant musk of her sex,
Yearns, lipped in her litheness.
And the primordial serpent of infinite wisdom
Streaks the long lane of her body,
And makes for paradise.

                        But in the sigh of that entry
A long suspension seizes their nerves. And for a lingering moment
They meld again, each in the other,
The deep aura of contemplation still clinging about them,
The age of action only beginning.

As though loath to leave one love for a better
They breathe there a moment.
The long dark of their contemplation coils to its term,
And the dawn of action leaps in their loins,

For the deed to be done,
Out of the shape of their shared souls,
In the savagery of love.

And the man
Moves, and the woman she moves, and they quicken.
And the phallos swells, plies firmly forward,
A slow cumulative gaining of pace, a matching increase.
Freed from restraint the phallos shakes forward,
Running loose now like a swift loper, running in and in,
Tucking neatly, picking up points, a fecklessness,
A brisk forward furtherance in the joy of thrust,
And gaining, gaining, picking, packing,
The dark runner pacing, the headstrong racer.
And the woman works. In the long lapse of her love
All the juice of her lonesome body
Sinks and swirls to find deep center.
She is deeply clutched, truly seized; the well of her passion is all
    abrim.
Throbbing up below from improbable deeps she begins to gain.
Her heart sweeps, she throbs to the man's great rocking motion, she
    begins to flame.
Here and there in torso and plexus the nerves whip, fire like pitchpine
    flaming,
Little running gusts of it, the ball of the fire-van
Finds its shudder and starts to roar.

And suddenly the running is all alive and roaring within her.

And the taut phallos feels that fire, and leaps up speed, feeding it.
Now within them each twin pulsant centers, heart and groin, pound
    toward union.
Breasts fused and flattened, skin to skin and bound there,
Twinned bosoms a swelling of ardor beneath that breadth,
But the loins free, for the loins are their work, they crave liberation.
In the body of the man prone heart and flat phallos cry out together,
The supple back throwing the great cock forward,

144

Only heart and phallos, looping through in an interaction.
And so too in the woman, her clenched cunt flattens on the heaving
    man, for her vulva is free,
And it holds free, the suppleness of liberation, the swivel of con-
    course,
The flaming heart and the floating cunt,
The loose hips thudding, coupling into a free-making flight.

And they make to move, they make motion,
Are savagely joined, are free in action.
Now they are all one body, for this is the actualization,
The whole term, the stung merge of spirit and flesh,
Souls long since joined in the godly rapture,
The bodies now are all for action, and the hips hitting.

And the man keeps himself, a freedom of force, and serves the
    woman.
And serving her richly she has aplenty, and begins to go.
All through her spine that flexed compelling force is going.
The fire aroar in her hips and her headstrong body,
The stroked buttocks stepping, pelvis tossing and floating,
Her strong legs quicking, strong young torso flexing forward and
    back,
Taut belly doubling, she is now all form, all fit and freeness.
Caught to the coign, coming into her own she begins to gain.
And the man, holding, lets her gain,
Gives her a bit of rein as she wills and the spur stings her.

And beside his ear her mouth makes now a silent sob, and of her
    pounding heart a gasped oath.
(The holocaust in her loins, gust of her body, the lava boiling out of
    her tarn.)
And this oath of her heart sends the signal leaping along his nerve,
    makes a fierce upkindling.
And he starts to drive, to overtake; is driving now, he is freely riding.
She is just out of hand and he lets her go.
As she goes he gains, her loins low now and coming up out of

procreant depths,
The breasts fused and the hearts oned,
But the hips resplendent, supple, magnificent in the liberating arc.
The whole bed it seems is starting to soar, her arms hugged crisscross
    about his back
Or flung wildly betimes around his neck to shag his head on her
    oath-sobbing mouth.
Or she sends them momently downward to thrust the small of him,
    the neat back,
Press him closer where her wonder is.

Where wonder drives and glory is and her whole existence.

And now in the gain he overtakes, and bearing her up he brings her
    on,
The sheer insuperable tensibility, the strength of the phallos.
It has the mastery between them now, the unspeakable force,
Nothing obtains but its total night, the sole immensity.

Consumed in its vaster dimension
He pours into her all his mustered strength, male, the ancient poten-
    tial.
And he goes, in his onrush now all is giving,
Knees, legs, thews, loins, back, brawn, body,
Everything he is and more than he is.
For in his call-up of resource he gathers behind him all he holds:
The nodes of his life, the myriad factors that fashioned his fate,
And all nature:

      Beyond him the River,
And beyond the River the continental mass,
And beyond, the humped hemisphere, somnolent, awash like a whale
    on its primal sea,
And beyond the hemisphere the globed earth, female,
Bathed in the white sun's seminal flare.
And beyond the sun all the orgastic fire of the stars,
Seething and seeding down the web of space—

Each one is seized,
As the God so seizes in the act of existence, in the swept fire,
The excellence of the creative act,
So that with every drive, the plunge struck forward,
As the phallos head thuds the nerve-centered womb, that thrust
Creates the Real. It is all
Made over: by the phallos,
In the phallos-thrust; at the entrance of the womb.
All, all is engaged in the man-driving thrust,
Pounding concentration, a stunning rhythm,
A terror of pace, an enveloping thunder,
A wind out of nowhere, blown through the holocaust of blood,
And its light snuffed.

And each reaches out of their own apexity, and at the ultimate peak
Match motion. And at their motion matched
Suddenly the world
Cracks, the phallos
Slams home, slams the ultimate stroke.
And the universe splits, the touched-off tinder,
Fired by that blazing torch,
Detonates all the tamped and pounded down empacted intensity,
All power compressed there; she bursts into brilliant uprush, a sear-
    ing crescendo,
Skyrockets, soars at the apex, one utmost instant, explodes—
And then tips down, his thousand flashes of splashed fire streaked on
    her sky.
And she veers, goes crazily out of control,
Consciousness erased, the lyric mouth
Shaped on the sole scream of ecstasy, and the throat
Ringed on the zero of the female idea
She knows at the core,
Soul and body
United on a single point,
Shears dizzily down.

But no. The great rivering phallos

147

That established her there will not let her drop.
Rather it holds her, sustained on the passional trajectory, a force
        unbelievably above,
Not of earth, stepped down from stars,
Like the meteor of which it has become a type,
In the incommensurate majesty of its own objective, it bears her on.
And seizing it up in the closed spasm of her survival
She saves herself, she hugs it, she coils, her up-coiling spine
Forcing the engorged maw of her split body
On the terrible piston still stuttering within her,
Clutched on the phallos, the total female grip, the fierce vise of her
        body,
And her teeth nailed in his neck. Only her heels, spasmodic,
Clipped above in a closed convulsion,
Hammer his back.

        And now the nexus.
Still lifting, upclimbing on the ascending trajectory,
The phallos becomes a thing insuperable, as much beyond him as her,
The consuming clutch of her utter outgoing spasms his own.
He hangs, one agonizing instant, in the stretched ultimate of his
        gripped embrace,
Beyond time, aware only of the majestic dynasty in which he exists,
And the enveloping gout of female propensity
Fastened upon the core of his being,
Out of which he completes himself, or is indeed completed, and hence
        is absolved.

He hangs in the ecstasy of recognition, and then erupts, explodes in
        answer.
Out of the phallos pour all the volatile myriad millions, the inches of
        existence,
Universal galaxies swept through the megaphonic loins,
The thundering mouthpiece buried in her womb, shut there,
The terrible shout of all finality
Wrapped in her flesh.

        And the finger of God

Inscribes on the uterine wall of night
Its prophecy of life.

And they fall.
The great cities of their mutual awareness are earthquaked under.
All over their sky the apocalyptic constellations
Shatter and fall down, splashing a million meanings
In the depths of their night.

Released from the phallos's august dominion
They collapse into the mutually fallen and gasping heap of their love,
And they pant, in their humanness restored,
Their mouths moaning little cries of reprieve,
A shivering delirium hovering about them,
Seething and twinging the inches of their flesh,
Their eyes on no dawn, night closing over them,
Giving back into darkness, going out.

And the sprung phallos.
Drenched of its deed, outblown, utterly divested,
It pulses into her sovereign keeping
The deep benediction of seed.

Under scant stars,
Smooth black water, bearing south,
Urgent, evocative, running with thunder,
The River.

      Far down its length
The great snake-headed delta
Plunges into the Gulf.

    *

And the sea, merging in on the land,
Moves through weft shallows, the tidal inlets and the creekmouth
    fens.

Rising upriver it washes through rich alluvial valleys, backwater
     bayous,
Taking the farms and the lush savannahs, possessing the domes of
     sentinel buttes.
At the clefts of rivers tall palisades murmur a moment and then slide
     under.
Beyond them glimmers the lift of the land: vast undulant prairies and
     high plateaus,
The upland benches and the granite slopes, all tremble and subside. At
     the last
Remains alone the great snow-hooded chain of the Rockies, backbone
     of the continent,
One luminous ridge, rippling pale stars. It hovers a moment,
Aloof, majestic, gathering about it the dream and memory of its vast
     domain,
Watershed of the western world, then soughs and sinks in.

                    *

Enraptured on floodtide,
The man and the woman, two continents athwart,
Return to the shoals of their contemplation.
In the drenched flesh, in the fabric beyond the flesh,
They have touched transcendence, a syzygy
Greater than wonder ever could know.
There is nothing other.
Passed to the realms beyond regard they have spanned distinction.
The great emptiness, binding disparate essences together,
Grasps them in its utter existence, quenches.
All the violent extremes falter and fade out.
Only the vaster measure, that exists beyond borders,
Possesses it all.

               Far back on the bed
The man and the woman, mouth slack on mouth, the deep sigh of
     deliverance.

In the wells of flesh the spent phallos, loosening,
Regains its selfness, its great deed done.

                                        It lies in her flesh
Like the prone hero, spent at the zenith of his awesome deed,
Subsumed in the shrouding folds of conquest,
In the halls of death.

                    Now and again
The man stirs a little and touches a little,
Stirring back on the memory of comprehension,
A hand cupping the breast.

The limbs withdrawing, phallos slowly retreating,
Withdrawing and receding from out of her flesh, instinctively return-
        ing.
The labial cleft slowly relinquishing, soughing to deliver back its
        burden,
The matted hair of the male and female
Mutually untangling, strand by filament
Slowly untwining.

                    They lie at last
Side by side, the entranced limbs together, collapsed on the bed.

The woman, back to the earth, facing the total experience of night,
Her legs atwain, her elbows
Utterly lax at her side, throat swelled up,
The white columned enactment, and the face
Drenched with completion.

And the man lies along her, his palm
Placed on the somnolent mound of her being, the cleft of her body,
Her well of existence, the fount of all substance.

And the woman takes up the spent phallos, and her palm possesses it,
The coiled serpentine mystery, the foiled lightning inert now,

Its primordial wisdom captive in her hand,
The enkindling godhead, spent of the splendor, possessed at her wrist,
The great glans trailing its fine seed, slowly in slumber, exhausted.

And she holds it, sighing, stirring her loins a little,
Where the hand of her husband
Cups the deep seat of existence, her body's cleft, the nuclear essence.

And night possesses.

Only the vast seas awash.
Only the elemental shores drowned under.
Only the night . . .

                    And they touch.
Touchings, traces of essence,
Occasional resurrections of consciousness
Flitting back to comprehension,
Reestablishing momentarily the primacies of fact,
Little rockheads of awareness, awash in the vast ocean of night,
The lapse of repose.

                    And the woman stirs.
The right leg curved at the side of the man, his loins bending above it,
Her left knee updrawn, the arch of instep
Laid at the knee, or there where the thighs
Join together, and the low mound is nestled,
Its matted tangle of sexual verdure
Under his hand, hub of awareness.

Out of the Self into the Other.
Out of the Essence into Existence.
Out of the Many into the One.

The vast flush possesses them.
The Many are no more.

This, the great Cloud, erasing distinction,
The contemplative's
Speechless gaze, vast murmur of love:
In this they abide.

                    And the man stirs.
His mouth sighs on the woman's, he lies on his side,
His proneness against her, his inert loins
Drooped on her flank, his left arm, under her neck, looped through
        her armpit,
The left palm cupped on her breast, its tensile resilience
Nippling between the second finger, nuzzling the third.
His right hand stirs on the mound of commingling,
Where the body forks and unites, and her oneness is,
The clean smell of their sex
Rare in the air.

The myrrh of that rapture, outflowing, suffuses the musk-drenched
        bed.

And out of immenseness, flux upon flux, the vast dynasties give back,
Gathering again from the folds of night,
Lifting here and there the great heads of their mountains out of the
        sea.
The moon grows in the sky, a few stars glimmer,
The great Cloud rifts its denseness.
Far down its ray the planet of the East gleams and looks earthward,
And on the low muffled line of horizon
Dawn trembles toward being.

                    She lives. Her belly
Undulates toward the sky, the navel
Set in its small oasis, her ribs faired back from the solar plexus,
Supporting the high sustaining breasts.
Between her shoulders the neck rises into the chin and the delicate
        jaw,
Her eyes closed in slumber, the brow brushed back to the hair's

helmet, the long tresses
Dividing and crowning the shapely skull. At the foot of the bed
Her right foot, ankle outturning, points toward the west.

And the woman touches the man.
Her hair, swept over her shoulder, lies spent on his neck.
Under his fingers the breasts' suspiration lifts and falls.
On the moon-bodied mound, the pubis, the right hand of the man
Stirs to the lift of her loins, lifting in stir of spent desire,
Redisposing the hips on the latitudinal bed.
Her skin, cool now, svelte, filled with the kept lustre of passion,
Electric with being, takes the newest air of morning.

She opens her eyes.
The phallos, spent yet in her hand, is sunken in slumber,
A moistness yet from its fallen tip traces her thumb.
The deep memory of its mastering splendor
Stirs in her thought; in her love she lifts it.
And the phallos, heavy with godhead, lifts in her hand,
It stirs in resurrection.

The great head of her husband lies plunged in sleep.
She breathes, a deep sigh of renewal, the infinite
Satisfaction of life. And life wakes in her womb.

The man stirs, the father.
On the body of woman, in the body of the bride, the man makes her a
    mother.
In the womb of the mother
The father makes himself son. In the body of his bride
The bridegroom repossesses his mother, achieves his fatherhood.

Thesis: antithesis: the mind distinguishing only to unite.
Antithesis: synthesis: grown back into wholeness.
The syzygy of the paired opposites
Replete with oneness. Man and woman
Envelop their meanings, subsume their essences.

Out of emptiness, the abyss of Godhead,
Back from the Many into the One.

Out of the Many, back from the One,
They grow, they gather, they become, they are.

Gazing again into each other's eyes,
The vastness of love that once overwhelmed them
Finds its focus.

       In the deeps, on the worlds of each other's flesh,
Into the skies of each other's spirit,
Upon the seas of each other's blood, out of the earth of each other's
    bones,
They look, they behold, they recognize, they know.
From the rolling waters of night the continents emerge.
Under the eastern glimmer of light
The River runs to the sea.

     *

And far out in the dawn the first bird of morning opens his beak.
In the tops of pinetrees the light wind hovers,
On faraway peaks air quickens in motion, revolving the night.

The woman trembles in sleep.
In the cup of her hand the great glans
Nuzzles her wrist, its total dimension
Spent of its seed.

The man, his mouth a moan, the head plunged earthward, dreams
    darkness.
In his dream the body of woman lies open before him, quiescent, a
    total love.
He sees her eyes, possessed of an infinite wisdom, turned in wonder-
    ment upon him.
He reads there her love. She shapes her mouth for a token, one

155

syllable of regard.
He smiles and assents.

By the side of the man
Woman opens her eyes. She looks out at the waning darkness,
The great mystery, a hushed recurrence of dawn.
Beyond their house the prime river-might is bourning down to the
    sea.
The water, a yellowish cast in the early light, tosses and goes south,
Its strength flexing at center, portentous and vast.

A skimmer, dipping low on the tensile surface, snaps up a fly.

The husband stirs; he opens his eyes.
He looks in the lids of his wakening wife.
Her lips move, the little mewing motion of kissing.
Lifting his head he kisses the mouth of his wife.
Her hand stirs on the phallos.

On the mound of his love the hand of the husband is cupped in
    relaxment.
His fingers thread the sensitive hair.
She has delivered herself all up to him now, in her need of wholeness.
Without him what is she? A need and a wanting.
She knows herself in his total completeness, the meaning he makes.
Her hand lifts up the phallos and lets it fall.

He is hers, possessed of her. In her
He discovers his solitary essence, he finds himself.
She creates. In herself, out of himself, she makes him be.

They stretch. In the pits of their arms the firm hair,
Fragrant with sweat, cools to the dawn.

He kisses her armpit,
Nuzzling into her fragrance there, the pure musk of her body.
She stirs, moving her hips, flexing the left knee and the thigh, the leg

lifting.
His hand strokes the deft inside of her thigh, goes back to the pubis.
Over her shoulder the skein of her hair lies lax on his neck.
Their eyes slake silence.

Awake now, he turns beside her.
The phallos stirs and is stretched, a new strength fills it. But the man
Abides. She herself declines to excite him:
They know how to wait.

She cups the phallos in her left hand,
Her fingers explore the weft at its root, its head nuzzles her wrist.
She takes in her fingers, curiously with wonder, the soft seed-sack,
    the scrotum
Folding and flexing in her hand.

The sun, strong now, reaches low through the window.
Outside, birds flit in the trees.
Small beasts of dawn are alive in the thickets.
The great River, luxuriant and complete, bears south to the sea.

The man kisses the woman.
His hand on her breasts jostles them strongly,
A full manful motion.

Releasing the phallos she plunges a hand through his tousled hair and
    drags down his head,
Kissing the slacked mouth, a strong buss of enjoyment.
She stretches again, arching her back, the slow body wakening,
Yawns deeply, drops in a sudden flex of relaxment, and scratches her
    flank.

The man stirs; he looks out at the world.
He rises on elbow, swinging his legs off the rumpled bed.

The dawn is upon them.

Deep in her body the new-given life
Already stirs growth.

                    She sits up beside him,
The great mop of uncoiling hair fanned on her shoulders.
Stooping to dress he looks out the window.
The sun lies firm on the wide earth and the River runs.
Far back at its root the Rockies shimmer the morning light, high
     snow-water trickles.
Somewhere ahead, in the vast savannahs, the River bends to the sea.

Kissing his neck once more she smiles.
He answers her, his gaze replying, his lips saying so,
His mobile face speaking his love.

She lets him go, smiling.
And smiling he stands up beside the bed, and pulls on his shirt.

BOOK FOUR:
THE HAZARDS OF HOLINESS
1957-1960

JACOB AND THE ANGEL

And Jacob was left alone; and there wrestled a man with him until the breaking of the day. And when he saw that he prevailed not against him, he touched the hollow of his thigh; and the hollow of Jacob's thigh was out of joint, as he wrestled with him. And he said, "Let me go, for the day breaketh." And he said, "I will not let thee go, except thou bless me."

—THE BOOK OF GENESIS

His mother's fondness wrought his father's frown.
Supplanter from the beginning, struggler in the womb,
Heel-holder, the overreaching scion. She egged him on.
For her offense she saw him hounded out of home
Nor lived to look again, ever, on the longed-for face.

Well warned if rudely, weaned, the outflying son
Beheld the laddered angels in their intercourse with earth,
His first liberating sign, if late. In that deliverance,
Freed from the mother's death-hug, trended east,
And over the well-dark water gazed on the sudden bride.

But guilt had split him. Deep down the offended father
Lived on symbolic in the maid's evasive sire,
His mother's brother. Duped by the blear-eyed sister
In his bed, trickster out-tricked, he swallowed gall,
And suffered the serfdom of those sweat-compounded years.

Suffered and loved and prospered. Even in bondage
His talents stood him well: the slat-eyed ewes
Bred neatly, flocks flourished, his wealth was won.
Seizing his sunk soul force he broke for the border;
Faced out the father on the slope of Galaad.

Faced, forced the offender, and sudden victor, saw
The signifying angels at the Camps of God,
Mark of the second liberation. Father-freed,

He gathered up the measure of his mind, turned home
To offer restitution, expunge the ancient debt.

But fear still fouled him. The raw unreckonable guilt
Sapped at his manhood, guttered his whole-felt strength.
Off there the beaten brother mustered up his men.
How could the exile know but that the wound
Had sown a poison, wrathful, had festered the sullen years?

And falling on his face he prayed to God, and rose
Dividing family from family, setting flock from flock,
Over the ford of Jaboc. Shivering he watched them
Breast the dark water. All was committed now. Alone
He waded the freshet last in the apophatic night.

But hold. Tall by the boulder, athwart the torrential flow
Spied out one shadow menacing that ford.
Esau? Stalking perhaps the hazardous creek-cross,
To there assail the pilgrim in his pass,
Bash out his brains, usurp his anguish-garnered hoard?

Fear! Fear! Midstream the exile wavers,
Tortured by guilt, doubt-wrung, his guts all gone.
About his loins the death-dragged water seethes,
Creeling his doom, and the grainy flints of fate
Sift and suck out beneath his terror-fastened feet.

No help. No hope. Nothing. If this be Esau
Then Jacob meets his star. Brother to brother,
Shadow to lipless shadow, the twin identities
Confront. Deep down his spirit gropes. Desperate
He grapples that stranger in one fierce convulsive rush.

This, then, at last, the divine engagement.
Who wrestled with his brother in the womb
Wrests now the angel. The years go down tumultuous
Beneath his trampling feet. O mother-favored son

What deed of truth did all those phantasies prefix?

One queasy crime—and the score-long exiled years!
How many mockeries of the inscrutable archetypes
Must we endure to meet our integration?
Is it fate or merely malice that has made
Us overreach our brother in the burdened womb?

Is it fate or merely malice that entraps
Us early in our own self-hugging hearts,
Darlings of our mother's doting eye, to steal
The kindly blinded father's foremost blessing,
Too soon seize up the giddy promises of God?

Fatality or malice, either-or, that curse
Curses us cold. We in our sin will never see
The glad, long-looked-for land. Mother-duped exiles,
Skewered on our father's guilt, we learn, we learn
Too late to face the angel, engage the hidden God.

All night they fought. All night the home-starved son
Turned in torment in the angel's withering grasp,
There on the trampled weeds by the root-grown shore
Where the sullen winter freshet, flushed with grit,
Rushed by like passion in the black prophetic night.

What vast eternities hang here contained?
What conflicts down the long genetic line
Suffer their extirpation in the wrestler's stance?
High overhead the great globed constellations
Hover like circling birds above the struggled heads.

And far down the planet's dark nocturnal side
The night-wombed nations murmur into birth.
His sistered wives, confused and terrified,
Twin aspects of his dark divided life,
Crouch in the weltering night and moan for his reprieve.

Dogged the man fights on, grappled wrist and knee,
And when the dawn blurs in the time-pressed angel
Glances at the east and makes to go.
But the exile, obdurate, closed in the unremitting
Grasp, exacts the specific blessing that he needs.

The man has won. Standing at last alone
He staggers on the twisted thew, if not
Invincible at least undaunted. This anguish
In the sinew is his sign, his final liberation,
Seal of the smiling God, the serene benediction.

Hurt but truly healed he sways, who seized
In the heart's black hole the angel of intellection,
And rose renewed, in the soul's great upsurge shaped.
His painful deprivations all converge
To make the anguished synthesis of his perfection.

And is called Israel, striver with God, and limps
Into the light of the huge ingesting sun, and meets
The long-feared brother: who beholds a saint,
Measured in the furious siege of grace, and seeing
Weeps on that placid neck, kisses the God-calmed face.

ALL THE WAY TO HEAVEN

All the way to heaven is heaven.
                                            —ST. CATHERINE OF SIENA
And the Lord said to Satan: Behold, he is in thy hand.
                                            —THE BOOK OF JOB

All the way to heaven
Is Hell. And the devil posts it.
Prince of this world, devourer of souls,
Whose mandate keeps the very inches of our lives
In specious fee, we trudge, we trudge, stumble year-long
Limp through the ancient shires of our affliction,
Tormented . . .

Dust of the earth
Is all we have to walk with
And the dust is his.

Dust of the earth
Stacked to the mortal frame.

Dust, and the dust is his,
Given him, his private use,
His plaything, his horrible
Doll.

Man walks: a demon
Smirks, crouches
On his shoulder,
Clots his ear.

Man sleeps: a demon
Hulks, debouches

In his brain,
Reeling the motion picture of his dream

From mad to vile.

Man loves: a demon
Sulks, slouches
In his heart,
Kindling a winy rancor . . .
Love strips, lascivious.

Oh, brother-devil!
Shadow and adversary!
My keeper!
Double of the heart's imago!
I do acknowledge!
I do concede!

Your virtuosity
Confounds my virtue.

Your foresight
Botches my insight.

Your prescience
Tortures my sentience.

Dabble your fretful finger in my blood, Hellhound!

I bear thy obscene vision in my breast
And tread thy mill with staves upon my neck!

A SIEGE OF SILENCE

A siege of silence? Thy meaning-moving voice
Hushed in the heart's crypt, thine eye
Shut in unreckoning slumber—
God? God? What storms of the dredgèd deep
Your absence lets, the rock-croppage mind,
Kelp-girthed, sunken under swell,
All seas of the unislanded soul
Typhooned, hurricaned to hell!

God! God! A place of eels and octopuses
Opens down under! Hell-stench
Sulphurs the waters, the drench of madness
Gags my plunged head! Death's belly rips!
The Devil's ruptured fundament,
Fawning with reechy kisses,
Strokes my lips!

God, to purge the memory pure
What cautery is needful?
To ease the soul of rancor,
Quench its hate?
God, God of the paradisal heart
I wait!

PASSION WEEK

Christ-cut: the cedar
Bleeds where I gashed it.

Lance wound under the narrow rib.

Eve's orifice: the agony of Abel
Enacted out on the Tree.

Blood gushed
From the gash.

The Holy Ghost
Gusted out of the sky
Aghast.

Our Guest.

Bleed cedar.
Little cedar,
Lanced,
Axe-opened,
The ache of sacrifice.

Pour out,
As Christ,
Those pearls of pain,
Bequeathed.

O bleed
Little cedar,
Bleed for the blooded Heart,
For the pang of man . . .

The earth's
Old ache.

ZONE OF DEATH

Wind is not nigh.

No Holy Ghost,
Spirit outspilt,
Burnt this charred day.

What sin did this?
Could I?

Hot light blares.
Stars, outblistered now,
Mark time, extinct.

Night might bring
The seasonal constellations
In its sphere,
But night is nowhere.

Sun. Sand.
The noon-crazy jays
Cackle and gibber,
Jar on the gritted ear.

Dawn sneaked in unsmelt.
No wine, no water here.

Now the lance-riddled man
On yon pronged tree,
Stretched in the death-tread there,
Opens his executing eye
And gibbets me.

WHAT BIRDS WERE THERE

Wheresoever the body is, thither will the eagles be gathered together.

—SAINT LUKE'S GOSPEL

Two magpies under the cypresses.
And what birds were there then I wonder,
To make a graveness in the afternoon
When the nailing was done to the cross hilt,
The man-act centered on the heart of God, irrevocable?
Sparrows, to be sure, scratching about in the street offal,
Yes, curb-brawlers, common as fleas,
Picking right and left for barley seed in the horse manure.
Doubtless a meadowlark off on a fence,
V-breasted, his splendor-drenched throat
Reaved on the spontaneous uprush
Of a rapture unremarked.
Or perhaps that treetop dandy the oriole,
Spinner of gestures, withdrawn now deep in his solitary covert,
His dulcet song, like rich contralto,
Unnoticed on that air.

Say rather, and more to the point,
Two gyrfalcons for outriders sweeping the cross quarter,
Circling, kleeing their strict sabbatical cries,
Imprecational and severe as executioners,
A curse on all triflers. Say further,
The mountain raven, malevolent prophet,
Utterer of virulent indictive oaths,
Imperious from the lodgepole pine,
Damnation drawn down out of the black beak inexorable.
Say too the appalled roadrunner,
Off in a fright scandalized over the stubble patch,
The town curs yelping after. Say most significantly
That grim gliding keeper of appointments, that dark
Ceremonial purist the vulture, a frown on the sky,
Methodical as an undertaker, adaptative

And deferential as the old woman of griefs
Who wraps up the dead.

But this does not mean, small birds of a feather,
That you, in your earnest beneficent presences,
Were somehow inapposite: linnets and speckled finches,
Fleet swallows, sheer swifts of the chimney;
Nor may it impeach your own most consonant
Purling evocative condolence, rain doves of the roof.
Better than those who thumbed sharp iron and plaited thorn!
Better than those who rattled dice for a stranger's shirt
And sponged galled water! Better than those
Who palmed hard silver to close a deal and slunk off after,
Too guilty to haggle! Oh, better by far
Than any of these were you, were you, flit messengers,
Arrived at that place all unbeknownst of what was toward,
But quietly there, not come but *sent*, keeping a tryst
After friend and foe had all alike gone over the hill,
Back down to man's dearth, man's glib and man's madness,
Nor left any light, the owl only upon the slab
To mourn the ruse when the moon sagged out, exhausted,
Her face demented, her jaw half gone,
Till the fierce star of morning
Pierced like the inner eye of God that scorning cloud,
Birthmarked that dawn!

SAINTS

Amen, amen, I say to thee: when thou wast younger, thou didst
gird thyself and didst walk where thou wouldst. But when thou
shalt be old thou shalt stretch forth thy hands, and another shall
gird thee, and lead thee whither thou wouldst not.

—SAINT JOHN'S GOSPEL

I who ravished a joy lost under my hand
The very rapine killing it.
Who stole for profit
What vanished that moment
I made it my own.
Who murdered for fear
What murdered me,
Its violence breaking out of my fist,
That suicide, my rape.

Man's heart!
What improbable depths are delivered up
When the seizure of faith grips the soul-string,
Bitted, heels it head over,
The long light thrown where darkness has dreamed
On untouchable snakes in their birth-nests,
Fosters the worm that gnaws on ever,
The unkillable core . . .

Man's heart!
To have known it indeed:
Confused, sensitive, cunning, depraved—
Most glorious!

God made it;
Man ruins it.
God-in-man work in purity and defilement
What neither alone could ever make be!

Not even God
Has power to force an evil act
But man does!

Every day he does!

I do!
Every day I do!

That work between us, God and I!
He the maker and I the destroyer!
Tearing down what he builds,
Besmirching what he pondered pure,
Profaning what he sanctifies!

O man!
Spirit screaming in the flesh!
Flesh screaming in the spirit!

Saints!
What secrets do you hold,
Pursed in your mummified lips,
Inscrutable back of the stiffly smile?

We thousands questing kneel here,
Beseech, our lips
Mumbling on invocation,
Twisting the rosaries of our supplication,
Knuckled hands, this desperateness,
These hope-dazed eyes!

You know!
We know you know!
You lived it through!
Fought up-ramp to the battlement,
Grasped the fell fiend on the pike-sill,

Rattled him till his teeth broke,
Flung him down all yowling into the dark descent,
Smashed all bloody damn him on the rocks below!

Yes?
Did you not so?
Was it not so done
When you did it,
Saints?

Saints!
Born out of sinners,
Sinners reborn!
In sanctity beatified—
That is all sainthood means,
Is it not,
Saints?

Your dead lips
Stretch on a secret
Not even you
May ever reveal.

Souls and warriors!
Great-hearted ones!
How may we hope to learn of you,
Of anyone,
For a course of battle
That can't be seen
Ever at all?
When what is relatable
Broke at a level beyond any ken?

Even you, even you,
Never really knew it, saints.
Stalwarts of the soul's war,
Prechosen.

But woke one morning
Dead and glorified,
Nobody more surprised than yourselves.

And looked back doubtless
As some thorn-torn climber
Pants at the peak-top,
Staring down in amaze
At the hell of cockle
He clambered through.

I've done that.
Looked back down all choked and bleeding
At what I crawled across,
Raking scorpions and poison-mouthed toads
Off my clothes as I stared.
I know that.

But now ahead
No cactus there nor any beasts,
No toads, no snakes,
No devils and no ghosts.

Nothing.

No thing. Not anything.

Not to be named, even,
Cursed at, grinned back against,
Invoked, knelt to,
Adored, denied, befouled or hated!

And nothing to love!

A blankness
Like neither night nor day

Confronts: the flat void
Of unrealization.

Before what will be
Is.

Before what might be
Can.

Like music you realize exists
But never hear.
Like terror you know alarms
But do not fear.
Like hope you know lives on
But can't conceive.

O soul!
O vast potentiality unprobed!
Be touched! Be opened!
Be moved! Be crushed!

God, withholding being
Just out of grasp,
Do something!
Kiss or kill
But move me!

Make me! Slake me! Back me! Break me!

A labyrinthine maze
That has no walls nor floor
Prevents.
A sea that has no wave nor depth
Foments.
A water without wet
Torments.
A life without a death

Dements.

God? Saints? Faith? Rapture? Vision? Dreams?—
Where?

I place my hand out.
Lead me!

I step, thus,
Lead me!

Lead me!

YOU, GOD

Nor any day gone,
Nor any night,
Measureless over the rimrock.

Nor those black imaginary suns
Roaring under the earth,
Roasting the roots of trees.

If I beg death, God, it is of you.

If I seize life, it is out of you.
If I lose, if I lose,
It is into you.

God of death,
Great God of no-life,
Existence is mine,
But you
Broach a nothingness
Breached out of nowhere.

Always you are not yet.

Deep in my guts,
Choked on oblivion,
Split, hearted on annihilation,
Caught through,
Smothered out,
A terror of emptiness,
Spat.

Immutable silence
Enormous over the snow mesa,
Enormous over the lava crag,
The wind-worked cloud.

My brain
Burns on your pierce.
My blood splits.
I shriek each nerve.

God!

Suck me in!

A FROST LAY WHITE ON CALIFORNIA

Thou shalt not offer the hire of a strumpet, nor the price of a
dog, in the house of the Lord thy God, whatsoever it be that
thou hast vowed: because both these are an abomination to
the Lord thy God.

—THE BOOK OF DEUTERONOMY

God. Spell dawns
Drained of all light.
Spell the masterhood of the means,
The flanges of extinction.
Spell the impotence of the numbed mouth,
Hurt, clenched on the bone of repudiation,
Spurning.

I grind it down. I grind on it.
I have yet to eat it up.

Crouched in my choir stall,
My heart fisted on stubborn revolt,
My two arms crossed on my chest,
Braced there, the cloak
Swaddling me round.

It is night.
I bore the darkness with my eyes,
Tearing it up.

Over the chapel the cold
Snaps on the roof,
Ringing with silence.
Two hours, spanning two inches of darkness.
I feel stars like hoarfrost prickle the tallness.
There ought to be a dawn.

"Do you think, O man, in that high

Toss of desire, that sheer
Aspirative hanker of yours,
What deeps go unplumbed?
Something within you is grinding its axle,
Spitting out sparks.
Stop for one moment,
Or ever so little,
And be assured you have read it aright.
That which is written between those flanges,
Spelled on the walls of the vascular heart,
Is your own scrawl.
What scars have you gouged on the stone of that cave?"

Fingered down in my deeps, I deny it.
What desolation, that depth!
Who says so!
What secret, that scrivening!
My own business, you.
Leave me alone.

"Do you think," cried God, "to have spat in my face
Driving me off that easily?
I ask you nothing not accorded a dog:
One glance of recognition.
To own what I am.
Which is you.
I am your image!"

The dark held through.
The stars, frozen, spit seeds in the sky.
I thought giant Orion,
The club-tossed arm,
Hurls over the house.
At ground level the frost
Gnawed at, bit tree-trash,
Loose leaf-stuff.

"I will not quit you," cried God, "for we are inseparable!
Do you hear? My name
Is carved on your heart,
There among the graffiti,
In capital letters.
That is my gash,
The struck brand,
The wound you made in your violence.
It will never heal.
You do not know how much I am you:
The other side of your face,
The back side of your body.
I stand between your shoulders.
I am that void behind your eyes
When you can't think!"

I wondered about the dawn, where it could be.
I sensed the wind veer south and west.
Two days it had held
To die in that quarter.
And in such death, out of that clear, frost fell.
Now the choir
Hung black and empty,
Hell's belly.
I felt the new wind, south,
Grope her tonguing mouth on the wall.
What does she want, this woman-wind?
She is trying to rain.

"Never forget," cried God, "I am your slave!
Call me and I come.
Curse me, I cannot quit.
I have never renounced.
Do you know what I am?
I am your woman.
That is my mouth you feel on your heart,
Breathing there, warming it.

I am more. I am your dog.
That is my moan you hear in your blood,
The ache of the dog for the master.
I am your dog-woman.
I grieve a man down,
Moan till he melts."

There was a rustling of winter-scarred weeds in the gutter.
It was winter, midwinter.
It was night, midnight, past midnight.
It was the dawn night. The scars in my heart
Were gashed by a terrible hand.
I clenched my heart on that gash.
I cursed.

"You are of flesh," cried God, "that is your light!
The shimmering sensitivity of the nerve.
Not I!
No brain to think with!
No nerve to think through!
I am dog in that I follow,
Woman in that I love.
Seek me!
In the heart of your disgust,
The germ of your revulsion,
The glint of truth impacted in your terror.
Invade me!
Flee that Luciferian
Light of the brain,
Pride of your life!
Down! Down! Behind! Below!
Quick! I am gone!
I, woman, moan against the bars.
I, dog, bay against the dawn."

I raised my head.
On such a night, long ago, when I was a boy,

There would have been a rooster
To rip the silence with a murderous yell.
I heard the wind turn west, southwest.
I said to myself: Do you think it will rain?

"Do you want it to," cried God, "and what for?
This ground is frozen.
Frost has locked hard on it now for too long.
The seeds are all tight.
Their lips are sealed.
They wonder when it will come a change.
They are like you."

I jerked back my hood,
Fighting the ache of my bones.
I am a fool.
Birds stirred out there in the crotches of bushes.
What red-breasted linnet will throat that dawn,
His voice a thorn?

"I have nothing to conceal," cried God, "from those deeps of your
        passion!
Why should I lie?
Read your own hate if you would know.
Would I squander blood on such as you if I didn't mean it?
Bah! I am always in earnest.
My hunger is plain as the pang in your gut.
Feed me! I am you!"

Was this a dream,
Some phantasy of anguish?
I crouched in my stall all night.
It was winter, midwinter.
A frost lay white on California.
I felt stars crack blue in my brain.

"I ask nothing," cried God, "that you wouldn't accord a dog!

I told you that!
The sheerest recognition.
That I do exist.
That I am yours.
Close your eyes now and be what I am.
Which is—yourself!
The you who am I!''

The roof of the chapel split up the sky,
A tree-wedge in a stump.
I felt the cold stitch my bones.
I should be in bed.
This is a fool to knock about here in the frozen hour,
Champing my teeth like a chittering ghost.
Who do I think I am?

''Who, indeed,'' cried God, ''when you think what you think?
Ask me who, I will tell it!
How far do I have to go?
Look! I crawl at your feet!
I, the God-dog!
I am all woman!
I eat from your hand!
Feed me. All I ask is your heart.
Am I that ugly?''

The light woke in the windows.
One by one the saints existed,
The swords of their martyrdom healed in their hands.
The linnet opened his voice;
He blistered his throat on the seethe of that rapture.
The suddenness split my skull.

''No pride!'' cried God, ''kick me I come back!
Spit on me I eat your spittle!
I crawl on my belly!
When you have gutted this madness

Drop down on the ground.
I will lick your hand."

That was the moment the dawn dragged in,
The cloud closed. It had slid from the sea,
Almost a sneak. I stood up in my stall,
Flung off my cloak. I heard the rain begin.

It was falling on the roof,
A slow spilth of deliverance,
Falling far, very far.

It was falling, I knew, out of the terrifying helplessness of God.

Into the frost,
Into the frozen crotches of the bush,
Into the feather of the singing bird.

Across the stuttering mouths of those seeds;
Against the sob of my tongue.

I AM LONG WEANED

*When I looked for good then evil came, and when I waited for light
then came darkness. My bowels boil, and rest not.*
                              —THE BOOK OF JOB

I am long weaned.

My mouth, puckered on gall,
Sucks dry curd.

My thoughts, those sterile watercourses
Scarring a desert.

My throat is lean meat.
In my belly no substance is,
Nor water moves.

My gut goes down
A straight drop to my groin.

My cod is withered string,
My seed, two flints in a sack.

Some day, in some other place,
Will come a rain;
Will come water out of deep wells,
Will come melons sweet from the vine.

I will know God.

Sophia, deep wisdom,
The splendid unquenchable fount:

Unbind those breasts.

IN THE BREACH

God!

The I-killer!
The me-death!

Rip me out!

Crouched in my womb,
Reality-butting head,
Mute-mouthed,
Gagged.

Breach!

Head-hunched,
Pelvis-pulled,
Heel-seized,
Sky-swung.

God!

My first scream
Skewers all night.
Far down
Earth's groan,
Gripe-gout,
The mother-grunt,
Gasps.

Where I?

God!

Caul-freed
I cry!

SLEEP-TOSSED I LIE

Sleep-tossed I lie,
Midnight stemmed under,
And the bloat moon
Shut in its sky.

Lord, Lord of these tangled sheets!
My wrestling's witnesses
Certify my heat.

I have lain long, lain long,
Long in thy grasp am lain,
Lord of the midnight watchings,
The monk's tongue-shuttered groan
And the hermit's heart-ripped cry.

Somewhere the wanton lovers keep
Vigils of fecklessness,
Their hearts
Bursted on passion
And the body's blade
Plunged deep.

And in that death find sleep.

But I? Long have I lain,
Long lain, and in the longing
Fry.

Sleep-smooth this brow.
Bless with thy rippling breath
These anguish-awkward limbs.

Grant thy surcease.
Toy me no more, Lord.
Lord of the midnight wrestlings
Keep the peace!

THE WORD

One deepness,
That mammoth inchoation,
Nothingness freighted on its term of void,
Oblivion abandoned to its selflessness,
Aching for a clue.

What clue?

Syllabled,
Shaken in its fixèd trance,
A far shuddering.

Who?

Blooms,
Subsumed in its sheer
Quality of inflection.

Endowed, the syllable
Focusing,
Determination conceives.

The concept
Borns of its pure consistency.

Not willed but perceived,
Not declared but acknowledged,
Yielded into the dimensional,
A salutation from the without.

Bearing within it strange liberties,
Consanguinations,
Dissolutions of oldness.

Rarer than the splendor it invokes,

More of wonder than its focal
Justness of perfection.

BLACK CHRIST

Heart not cry
Nor mouth moan?

I dread life,
The illusion.

I stand in life,
In light,
And woo death,
Dis-illusionment.

I dare not die,
Knowing not.

But I woo death,
Though I know not,
Know nothing.

Undeceive me, God.

Death is not ours,
We ourselves do not die:
Are killed.

Only you, O God, deliver.

Craving the cancellation
To possess the clarity,

I crave the truth
Beyond the illusion,
This nonexistence.

Let me exist,
Die unto the totality,
Half dead now
Of the nonexistent.

God, who can neither
Deceive nor be deceived
Is darkness,
My death.

Lucifer, who forever
Deceives and is deceived,
Is light,
My life.

Dark God, dark
God of death,
Thou art good—

Then *be* good,
Release.

Kill me.

Relieve me of the weight,
Relinquish me into the dearness,
Thyself,
That depth.

Redeem me into existence,
That darkness,
Thy love.

I beg thy kindness,
That dark
Unrapture.

Kill me.

I beg the lowliness
Of thy love,
That depth.

I beg thy kindness.

Merciful darkness,
The strict sweetness of terror.

Impeccable lovely fear,
The divine revulsion.

Holy unspeakable horror,
Beautiful annihilating pain.

The splendid and terrible anguishes,
The sublime insuperable hurts.

These the disenchanters,
Angels of deliverance,
Radiant sisters of mercy,
In their dread hands
Is borne the peace.

Send them, Lord.

Make me a marriage
Death, my master, my Christ.
Keep thy bed holy,
My cross.

Kill me.

My body, thy cross,
Make pregnant with thy seed,
Swell into definition,
Stalk of thy desire.

Black bridegroom,
Dear and dreadful Christ,
Deliverer,
Possess me.

Giddy I live.

Unable to die,
Drunk of the illusion,
The ruttish wine,
Lurching with deceit,
Unfit . . .

Giddy, I live on.

A CANTICLE TO THE GREAT MOTHER OF GOD

> *Now all good things came to me together with her, and innumerable riches through her hands, and I rejoiced in all these; for this wisdom went before me, and I knew not that she was the mother of them all. Which I have learned without guile, and communicate without envy, and her riches I hide not.*
>
> —THE BOOK OF WISDOM

Sometimes I dream you measured of bright walls, stepped on a hill
    and diademed with rose,
Sea-cinctured, the black wave-haunted wharves radialed round your
    hems, and the nuzzling tugs
Shunted like suckling spaniels at your piers.

All the resplendent bridges of your bays converge upon your heart to
    there deploy,
Dilated into streets, fanned to the outmost sectors, bloodlines of
    pulsant use that throbbing flow,
Serving the induct of all crafts and hallowed skills.

Trending into your colonnades at dawn, down from those air-girthed
    arches of the sky,
We pause in tremble, sleep-cozened but reprieved, stirred to the
    richening diastole.
Soaring on noon we sense it loudly replete, swelled to the stately
    tempo, augmented to the day-drummed dance,
Pace of the proudness, an opulence subsumed, the strident fluting and
    the resonance of blare.
Sinking toward dusk we drink a slowed, more moded music, muted, a
    hushed convergence, a deep relapsed repose.
In all the hinterlands about the trains come nosing home, mallowed
    of late light,
Shrilling their long crescendos, creaming with racing lamps the fast
    ingathered gloom.
Night is your nuance. Listening we hear the wild seabirds, flittered

like intuition through your coolest thought,
Falter and then fly on, seeding steep sky, the beacon-raftered verge,
South-sought, mewling one plaintive meed, a tremulance of plight,
before they pass,
Reflashing on pale tips the birth-reverted instinct of all trek.

Hidden within the furlongs of those deeps, your fiery virtue impreg-
nates the sky, irradiant with wisdom.
You are Byzantium, domed awesomeness, the golden-ruddy richness
of rare climes, great masterwork of God.
Kneeling within thy moskey naves, seized in the luminous indult of
those dusks,
We hold the modal increase, subsumed in chant, ransomed of the
balsam and the myrrh.
Keeping an inmost essence, an invitational letting that never wholly
spends, but solemnly recedes,
You pause, you hover, virtue indemnable, at last made still, a synth-
esis unprobed.
Checked there, we tremble on the brink, we dream the venue of those
everlapsing deeps.

But always there is a somethingness eludes us, Mother, city and
citadel,
Proud battlement and spire, croft, granary, and the cool, sky-
thirsting towers.
Obscure behind those nodes, those many-mingled lights, that wink
and then well up,
Pale opals on the movement of your breasts, or the navel-cuspèd
moonstone at your womb,
Always your essence hovers. The flashing glances of the sea belt you
about with brightness, blind our eyes,
And the famished senses swoon of that vaunted spicery.

For how could we ever know you wholly as you are, thou who are
clearly here so manifest of God?
Our coarseness keeps us pinioned of our nerves, while you, immacu-
late, conceived simplicity,

Subsume the inviolable instance. We are unworth, who shunt in
   stupor whelming at your breasts,
Rude shoulderers who sully what we seek, foul our sole good.

But you, that which you have, you give, and give it graced, not as it is
   but as we use it of you,
Dimensioned down to our foreboded taste, our thirst of need, filtered
   to our mereness and our plight.
We suck through sin. Our boon is that you are subsistent of the light,
   bringing the Light to us, whose darkness dams out grace.
Confirmed unto the kindness, gaped mouths of thirst, we tongue a
   milk like honey,
And know from whence it sprung, being yours, who never could taste
   the heaven-nurtured nectar that you use.

Believe us when we seek, Mother and Mercy, who in our lives are
   unbelievable,
All faithlessness of the flesh wrought flaccid, the stunt will burdened
   in the bone.
That need we nurse is sharper than our cry.
Through you alone, the Wisdom and the Womb, keen-creeps the
   child,
The visionary life fast-set against the acrid element, death's factual
   zone.

Clearly you are to us as God, who bring God to us.
Not otherwise than of those arms does grace emerge, blessing our
   birth-blank brow.
Wombed of earth's wildness, flank darked and void, we have been
   healed in light,
Traced to the sweet mutation of those hands, a touch closing the
   anguish-actual stripe,
Whip-flashed the sin, lip-festered on our soul.

But see: out of this too redounds your deepest motherhood;
As one unable to yield the child that utterness no child can spell,
She yet *subsumes* the truth, *is* the grave wisdom of her wakeful eyes.

Or else the child, callow-stumped and closed, never grows up to what
  deep knowledge is, completes its mode.
Our spirits, watchful, tenacious on their term, see to it only as it
  gleams in you, because of what you are,
The radiance on which the world's blunt might is closed, sharp in a
  singleness simple as any star,
Bright-bought, sheer as one nexus-seeding coal.

Hive of the honey, city and citadel, cathedral and cloister and the cool
  conventual keeps,
Receive us in. The anchorhold of heaven helms us on.
Hungered of that pledge we trample up the ramps limned of a vision,
Questing for what you smile of veiled in rapture mirrored in your
  eyes,
A solace deeper you said than all such clustered balms,
Pierced to a presence totaled on all truth, vaster than the prophet's
  dream descried,
And larger, if we believe you, even than your love.

IN ALL THESE ACTS

Cleave the wood and thou shalt find Me, lift the rock and I am there!

—THE GOSPEL ACCORDING TO THOMAS

Dawn cried out: the brutal voice of a bird
Flattened the seaglaze. Treading that surf
Hunch-headed fishers toed small agates,
Their delicate legs, iridescent, stilting the ripples.
Suddenly the cloud closed. They heard big wind
Boom back on the cliff, crunch timber over along the ridge.
They shook up their wings, crying; terror flustered their pinions.
Then hemlock, tall, torn by the roots, went crazily down,
The staggering gyrations of splintered kindling.
Flung out of bracken, fleet mule deer bolted;
But the great elk, caught midway between two scissoring logs,
Arched belly-up and died, the snapped spine
Half torn out of his peeled back, his hind legs
Jerking that gasped convulsion, the kick of spasmed life,
Paunch plowed open, purple entrails
Disgorged from the basketwork ribs
Erupting out, splashed sideways, wrapping him,
Gouted in blood, flecked with the brittle sliver of bone.
Frenzied, the terrible head
Thrashed off its antlered fuzz in that rubble
And then fell still, the great tongue
That had bugled in rut, calling the cow-elk up from the glades,
Thrust agonized out, the maimed member
Bloodily stiff in the stone-smashed teeth . . .

                                        Far down below,
The mountain torrent, that once having started
Could never be stopped, scooped up that avalanchial wrack
And strung it along, a riddle of bubble and littered duff
Spun down its thread. At the gorged river mouth
The sea plunged violently in, gasping its potholes,

Sucked and panted, answering itself in its spume.
The river, spent at last, beating driftwood up and down
In a frenzy of capitulation, pumped out its life,
Destroying itself in the mother sea,
There where the mammoth sea-grown salmon
Lurk immemorial, roe in their hulls, about to begin.
They will beat that barbarous beauty out
On those high-stacked shallows, those headwater claims,
Back where they were born. Along that upward-racing trek
Time springs through all its loops and flanges,
The many-faced splendor and the music of the leaf,
The copulation of beasts and the watery laughter of drakes,
Too few the grave witnesses, the wakeful, vengeful beauty,
Devolving itself of its whole constraint,
Erupting as it goes.

    In all these acts
Christ crouches and seethes, pitched forward
On the crucifying stroke, juvescent, that will spring Him
Out of the germ, out of the belly of the dying buck,
Out of the father-phallus and the torn-up root.
These are the modes of His forth-showing,
His serene agonization. In the clicking teeth of otters
Over and over He dies and is born,
Shaping the weasel's jaw in His leap
And the staggering rush of the bass.

GOD GERMED IN RAW GRANITE

God germed in raw granite, source-glimpsed in stone?
Or imaged out in the black-flamed
Onyx-open line, smoldered in the tortured
Free-flow of lava, the igneous
Instant of conception? As maiden-form
Swells in the heaviness of wold, sleeps
Rumped and wanton-bulged in the boulder's
Bulk, is shaped in tree-forms everywhere
As any may see: dropped logs, say, or those crotched
Trunks pronged like a reckless nymph
Head-plunged into the earth—so Godhood
Wakes under water, shape-lurked, or grave and somber,
Where sea falls, mocks through flung foam . . .

                                    Ghost!
Can this be? Breather of elemental truths,
She stirs, she coaxes! Out of my heart's howk,
Out of my soul's wild wrath
I make oath! In my emptiness
These arms gall for her, bride's mouth,
Spent-breathed in laughter, or that night's
First unblushing revealment, the flexed
Probity of the flesh, the hymen-hilted troth,
We closed, we clung on it, the stroked
And clangorous rapture!

                    I am dazed.
Is this she? Woman within!
Can this be? Do we, His images, float
Time-spun on that vaster drag
His timelessness evokes?
In the blind heart's core, when we
Well-wedded merge, by Him
Twained into one and solved there,
Are these still three? Are three

So oned, in the full-forthing
(Heart's reft, the spirit's great
Unreckonable grope, and God's
Devouring splendor in the stroke) are we—
This all, this utterness, this terrible
Total truth—indubitably He?

THE SONG THE BODY DREAMED IN THE
SPIRIT'S MAD BEHEST

*I am black but beautiful, O ye daughters of Jerusalem. Look not
upon me because I am black, because the Sun has looked upon
me.*

—THE SONG OF SONGS

Call Him the Lover and call me the Bride.
Lapsing upon the couch of His repose
I heard the elemental waters rise,
Divide, and close.

I heard Him tremble and I turned my head.
Behold, the pitiless fondness of His eyes;
Dark, the rapacious terror of the heart
In orgy cries.

His eyes upon me wanton into life
What has slept long and never known the surge;
Bequeath an excess spilt of the blood's delight,
And the heart's purge.

His lips have garnished fruits out of my breast
That maddens Him to forage on my throat,
Moan against my dread the finite pang
Of the soul's gloat.

He is the Spirit but I am the Flesh.
Out of my body must He be reborn,
Soul from the sundered soul, Creation's gout
In the world's bourn.

Mounted between the thermals of my thighs
Hawklike He hovers surging at the sun,
And feathers me a frenzy ringed around
That deep drunk tongue.

The Seal is broken and the Blood is gushed.
He does not check but boldens in His pace.
The fierce mouth has beaked out both my eyes,
And signed my face.

His tidal strength within me shores and brunts,
The ooze of oil, the slaver of the bitch,
The bull's gore, the stallion's famished gnash,
And the snake's itch.

Grit of great rivers boasting to the sea,
Geysers in spume, islands that leveled lie,
One snow-peak agonized against the bleak
Inviolate sky.

Folding Him in the chaos of my loins
I pierce through armies tossed upon my breast,
Envelop in love's tidal dredge of faith
His huge unrest.

But drifting into depth that what might cease
May be prolonged until a night is lost,
We starve the splendor lapsing in the loins,
Curb its great cost.

Mouthless we grope for meaning in that void
That melds between us from our listening blood,
While passion throbs the chopped cacophony
Of our stange good.

Proving what instinct sobs of total quest
When shapeless thunder stretches into life,
And the Spirit, bleeding, rears to overreach
The buttocks' strife.

That will be how we lose what we have gained,

The incremental rapture at the core,
Spleened of the belly's thick placental wrath,
And the seed's roar.

Born and reborn we will be groped, be clenched
On ecstasies that shudder toward crude birth,
When His great Godhead peels its stripping strength
In my red earth.

THE HAZARDS OF HOLINESS

I. THE BEHEADING OF JOHN THE BAPTIST

*And when the daughter of the same Herodias had come in, and had
danced, and had pleased Herod and them that were at table with
him, the king said to the damsel: "Ask of me what thou wilt, and I
will give it thee."*

—THE GOSPEL OF ST. MARK

John cried out—the excoriate definition
Of the invincibly sane. Naked adultery
And the greed of caste lolled notorious
In the royal sheets. The true tongue damned it.
Herodias, that corrosive female wrath,
Black grasp of the invidious breed,
Blanched, swore blooded reprisal.
But the Tetrarch, sensitive, winnowing those careful
Cross-fertilizing fears, that tease of the politic heart,
Smelled dangerous fire in the prophet's blood,
Checked his hand. Dungeoned deep, a claw of conscience
Repressed in the brutal heart of the State,
The Baptist dreamed implacably on,
Manacled but unmaimed.

        Salome danced.
Night of the tentative April moon,
A great guest-gathering, the air
Stung with the lingering shiver of winter
Zoned out of torrents and the freeze of caves.
She danced through the great encircling fires,
Among the lounging electrified troops.
This the Machaerus, steep fortress,
Stained with the gullied blood of invasion
And the howling native pang. Below: oblivion,
The salt-festered sink of the Dead Sea,
Sodom's crusted containment. She danced, pubescent,

In the heart's early ungovernable rage,
The fateful foot now perilously in quest,
Sentient of an indued splendor,
Path of the mortal wound.

                    "Give me the head
Of John the Baptist!" cried the violent girl,
Her eyes like an eaglet's blazing behind her unbrooched hair,
Mouth insolent with wine, throat panting
Those covetous gouts that howk toward murder,
The dauntless breast beating that oath up out of her blood,
Her sovereign demand. "On a plate! On a plate!"
She turned, imperious, her legs spread like a man's,
One naked arm distended, the savage bracelets
Aclash on her wrist. The Tetrarch, hooked,
Brooded momently over his cup of death.
Truly this grieved him. Looking plaintively round
He smiled, squirmed, lifted the hand of lifeless assent,
Concurred. Axe-chopped, the sublime features,
That had stared down priests and the brutality of queens,
Rolled in the mire, a girl's wild wish.
She had danced, had she not? Twirling her loose skirt,
The nubile thighs flashing the ringlets of excitation,
Flamboyant, the inflammable gestures of a crude sexuality
Nascently alive, a virgin gambling away her maidenhood
In the crouched animality of arrested stupration,
That thrust of blood in the heart's valves when treasure is spewed,
The toothed heels stuttering out a mirthless crescendo,
Rapacity unflexed, the impossible strut of childish excess,
Astute circlings of consanguinity, most ancient of inversions,
Blood calling to the blood.

                    Clash the spears, warriors!
Throw down those drinking goblets onto the stones,
You sunburned fighters, swart treaders of Asia,
Dirk-fierce drinkers of barbarous life—behold your own!
She danced. This is the night of her ruined girlhood.

208

She has earned it. She whirls the vesture of saints
For her scarves. The blood has bellowed. That Herodian lust
Burns already in the narrow groin, not long to be slaked.
On a plate, held high, tilted to the arrogant zest of life,
The great face of the innocent rides somberly in,
Black-mouthed, a terrible hole of condemnation cracked in the jaw,
Rebuking the confrontation of ecstasy and sin,
The dangerous edge teetering yet in those coinless eyes.
Into these disbelieving hearts, these faithless sallow souls,
The intrepid face thrusts its spleenless accusation, one final time.
Strutting, the outrageous, excessive girl confronts them,
Brandishing into the aghast male faces, flattened on the nexus
Of the opposed female will, her bloody pledge.
"Look!" her exultant eyes, her flaunting, indemnable lips
Exact it. "This is my trophy! I have asked
What none before me has dared! I dance henceforth
In the image of saints! I possess my desire!"

                                    Nobody laughed.
In the choked silence someone kicked a musician, and the zither
Screeched, a shrill hysterical bleat of masculine consternation.
Smoldering, her face flushed with aggression and contempt,
The umbrageous girl flounced menacing out, dragging her prize.
Her mother had won.

                          Northward on straw, beside another mountain,
Over against another sea, slept one, the latchet of whose shoe
Even the Baptist faltered to free. His dream dredged deep,
Seeing in time profanations more vile than the prophet's doom
Heaped on the platters of human forbearance.
Let the far tides fall. Let all the world's rivers
Run down to the sea. Jesus dreamed on straw
The inexorable prescience of the lurid fact.
The killed visage, clenched in the hands of the grinning girl,
Stared out the timelessness of the real,
Beholding nothing at all it had not foreseen
Many years back, in the womb, when the weak limbs,

Sphered in those lapsing waters of life, that fertile
Plangent sea, sprang the upsurgent body against those walls
As the truth shocked through, sharp in that trance
As a sent sign; as stones, struck under water,
Pierce to the swooning drowner's ear, rouse him urgently up . . .
So did John joy. In his wild womb-dance
He broke the stupor that obsessed the race,
Ancient of doom, the hauteur of the human province
Clamped like an ice cap on the surd heart;
The thaw of a sublimity that would soon, on his birth,
Unseal forever the sleep-dragged eyes, disburden
The breast of its fierce remorse,
And loose the vein of the tremendous tongue
That would thunder in the Redemption.

II. JUDITH AND HOLOFERNES

> *Then said Holofernes unto her, "Drink now, and be merry with
> us." So Judith said, "I will drink now, my lord, because my life is
> magnified in me this day more than all the days since I was born."*
> —THE BOOK OF JUDITH

Saint Judith crouched. About her loins
The instructed provocation of the harlot's intelligence
Or the widow's pang; the smoldering
Anticipatory inflection, flit nimbus of explicit consent,
Reckless awesomeness of the traducer's perversity
In the discipline of the saint.

Did a demon sodden the conqueror's brain,
Dredged with black wine, or was it an angel?
Holofernes, watching her fool with his cumbrous gear,
Would never know. She dragged the cutlass out of its sheath,
Gravely impressed, mocking over its honed edge,
Her dusked eyes darkening: "When the sword of my lord

Bites blood, in the mad battle, let my hope sing it home . . ."

She toyed with it, binding her scarf on the ponderous hilt
For favor, fondling the pendulous tassels she found there,
Curling finger and thumb round the thirsting point,
A spidery tickle. "Let it bring down the proud,
For which I have come to you, a woman's weakness
In the stitch of God's grace . . ."
She mocked her mouth at him over its edge,
The razor-stroked steel. "When my lord
Has pinked at last his terrible blade
I will quench my desire . . ." The conqueror grinned,
Lolling his muscular hams on their print,
The double indentation of crushed cushions,
Where his strong legs spread, and blinked sidewise.
"Promise," she mocked, "when my lord
Has blooded his terrifying blade, he will not forget
Where he learned his secrets . . ."

                        Outside in the camp
The cohorts slumped in sleep, collapsed on their weapons.
Above the bed, that deceptive keep of obsidional debauchery,
Where the masterplan of covert assault lay stretched and waiting,
A small lampflame dangerously flirted, sulked on its wick,
Twisting about like a snake's torso flexing to strike.
The great silks of the tent enveloped them,
In the voluminous silence of fortuitous stealth.
The camp lay dead. They alone looked to each other,
Contained in the gaze of engrossed betrayal,
And each banked passion—he, the inveterate rapacity
Of the nerve's conquisitional itch; she, the indominate rigor
Of the martyr's faith, who looks in the lion's distended jaw
And never flinches. For each, obsessedly fixed on the other's eyes,
This instant was all. And they swayed there, like mating snakes,
Loath to dispel it, too wise
In the stratagems of hate and desire
To seize too soon.

    "You understand," she said to him gravely,
"Something of what a woman is, I can see that."
(The light on her loins, the numinous fire
Fluxing out of her breast's slow fall.)
"I am not the first in my lord's life,
Being but a poor latecomer here,
Where others have lain, glad to make of their body a bed
For the chief's ease. Where are they now?
But how could they regret it? Perhaps my lord,
When he gives me leave, will find my gift,
Among his memorable accomplishments, not too
Utterly inconsequential, not too
Tiresomely trite?"

    She stirred, ruthless,
Projecting out of all her surfaces
The tyranny of her truth.

     And the conqueror smiled.
A woman of brains and sensibility, he respected that.
In his cagey respect, rooted down in his being's base,
The seminal propensity engendered in flux
Its thick provocation, the measure of the male.
Let her choose her time, a subtle mind
In a serpentine body, and when she chose it
The time, he knew, would be richer for that.

He drank deep, the aura of suggestibility
And the smoldering anticipation the sense stirs,
When a man expects what he holds already in the seething brain,
Excites the profile of deranged rapture,
Rush and roll of the blood plunged, the explicit
Female debouchment, so long allured and at last relinquished,
And the groin's crude grunt. He smiled, drinking again,
Compulsively, nursing his sodden tactical hunch,
Drinking and waiting, the sovereign passion

Spreading down in his deeps, a sleepy fire.

God uses the devil, Job proved that.
But does the devil use God? Holofernes, headless in hell,
Will twist forever on the demon's nail,
Crucified on the splayed tree of the sexual act,
Ejaculating out of the dismasted shoulders
The orgastic splurge of neuric excess.
Here, in his wantonest moment, the demon within him
Slumbered and slept, drugged down with wine,
Stupefied in the clog of diffused consciousness,
The guzzle of omnivorous thirst.
But the angel that lit her ecstatic face,
Limned with an exquisite ravishment,
Perfecting on the lips and the sinuous body
The delineaments of unspeakable gluttings,
The giddiness of delight in the shamelessness of grace—
That angel creates, and in the discrepant achievement
Outdoes the devil. Holofernes, divided on his own blade,
His swart head slewed back and chopped off,
Hewn loose in two hacks, and the bloated trunk
Stiffening in the cerement of his own arras,
His head balled up, stashed away in a woman's purse,
Never again to gloat in triumph on the proud neck
When battles are joined and maids deflowered,
Sings his own requiem, the terrified bellow
Of distempered blood. Oh, what angel of angels
Steeled the widow's wrist, purged it of weakness,
Hardened the voluptuous forearm for its zigzag crunch,
Endowing in the suave insinuative shoulder
The dint of Samson, and made all muscle the supple stern,
That had promised to tuck like a frisking minx
His wild uncircumcised pang—what angel enveloped her
When she squatted and struck, the cutlass
Slammed down and hacked through, the exposed jugular
Writhing back from the steel, as a garden snake
Frenzies under a woman's hoe

When she hews her greens in the wind-wade of spring—
All about the bull body, sacrificial,
The mithraic cadence of spent libido,
His legs asprawl, and the sprawled sex,
That would never again bleed a virgin's seal,
Dabbed with slick blood . . .

O ravishment of God
On the unspeakable face of the transfixed Jewess,
Awesome in its divine righteousness, its terrible truth,
To stand at last, like Salome alone, a man's head
Gripped in her hands!

Grieve you warriors!
Mourn your loss you great men of battle,
Blood-drunk dukes of carnivorous life,
Out there on the mesa, asleep on your spears,
Bedeviled by dreams of women and gods!
The moon steals over the stupefied camp, crisply,
And blesses at last the besieged city,
Softening the contours of warfare and weather,
Erasing the scars of violence, hate, the perverse tribulation
Of energic despair, atoning at last
In its delicate presence the harsh male madness
And the spoilage of man. The strange woman
Glides through the camp like a young goddess
Bearing her gifts, back through the thorn
And the desert gravel, over the flints,
Picking her way through camel dung and the urine of mules,
Drifting back to the beleaguered city that gave her birth,
Where the greybeard fathers, impotent,
Sit on their mats, invoking the inscrutable God,
Of whom in fact they have quite despaired,
To make in this hour some bland interpolation,
Discover within their obscure hearts,
Blind with the anxiousness of earth
And the libidinous rage that terrors their days,

The germ of rebirth, purging from their souls
The fraudulent thirst of the sword's conceit,
The furious grudge of His siege.

THE CONVERSION OF SAINT PAUL

And as he went on his journey, it came to pass that he drew nigh to Damascus; and suddenly a light from heaven shined round about him. And falling on the ground, he heard a voice saying to him: "Saul, Saul, why persecutest thou me?" Who said: "Who art thou, Lord?" And he: "I am Jesus whom thou persecutest. It is hard for thee to kick against the goad." And he trembling and astonished, said: "Lord, what wilt thou have me to do?" And the Lord said to him: "Arise . . ."

—THE ACTS OF THE APOSTLES

Jerusalem
Died in the dust.
They took the short route,
Up the river to Hippos,
Then straight through the desert,
Eight days, appoaching
At noon the heat-veiled city,
Oasised, green-cool in the desert,
The vernal gleam of an opal.

And coming out of that vastness the noonday sun
Blazed like the wrath of Yahweh, intense righteousness,
The downfalling stroke of noon.
Heat danced the meridian.
Bare ridges, steel blue, those ribbed
Horizon-haunters, swathed in the welter of ripples,
Air tingling, the stretched
Sizzle of hotness.

And the gaunt Pharisee, seeing it, stood in his stirrups.

Damascus, at last before him, the fragrant, plangent city,
Pearl-grey, cinctured about with pomegranates,
The slender stems of its date palms,
Lovely as a girl laughing by well-water,

Slim-vesseled virgin—but tainted, tainted,
Infected in the low place,
Crawling with christ-lovers,
Scabrous infestation . . .

Crash!
A brilliance so bright
The noon blanked black
Overhead where the sun was;
Intense radiance unwombed;
One lasting flash,
One fast unfaceable spasm.

The horse uprearing
Outspring from under,
Forked ears pronged
On the blinding intenseness,
The high pawed hooves . . .

Crash!
The clang of fallen metal, armor
Rang on the road, the flailed scabbard,
That loose-sprung blade, grit-grating,
Steel on stone.

Dust swallowed him up.

He lay enveloped, as one dead,
Stunned, swathed in dust,
Stupefied . . .

Saul! Saul!
Far off, beyond the Caucasuses, the innominate nightfall
Flows like music on the deepening steppes.
The homesick yak-herder, hunched against fatigue,
Dreams of the skin dusk of his yurt
And the slow hands of his hill wife.

Many the nights, many the nights of the love-rank bed,
And the blind suck of her mouth . . .

But for the Pharisee,
The bitten dust outside Damascus,
This night is new.
In his light-splintered brain
The local planets of his limited vision
Split and swept out,
Spending their ruin through the titanic vastness.
Shrill specks of consciousness,
Crying the railing pang of mortality,
They flecked and died out.
In that dream of oblivion
His ears rang with the terror of galactic silence:
The swung span of such lunar darknesses
The world never knows.

                    Saul! Saul!
Music of an exhalation
Softer than the murmur of love-pledges,
More vibrant than woman's wisdom
Or the sudden concourse of tongues,
Slower than the measure of migratory waters,
The lapse of cool oceans,
Or night-risen wind over fern . . .

                    Saul! Saul!
Sibilant, richer than the labial
Meaning of myth, a muted inflection;
Slower than the filmy lip-suck of waters;
As modulant as waterways
In their slowed convergence,
Through reed shallows,
Where the bulrush staves
Tugged at the tossing ark of Moses,
The dark drift of the Nile . . .

Saul! Saul!

In the red brain of the ruined prophet
The constellated pillars of enforced justice
Crack the hammers of retort and fall still.

He scrabbles his hands.
He claws his fingernails
Crazy in gravel,
His brute-blind, dust-dazed head
Addled in consternation.

He clutches his clothes,
He pants his pain-fed animality,
He gasps his moan.

They help him terrified up,
Limp him blind to Damascus,
The blistering heat
Beating him on;
His weak hands wilt,
His sobbing tongue
Blind and babbling,
His feet lurching the dust-blind,
Dog-dunged way.

Behind him the desert
Flattens its immemorial witness,
As sterile and lifeless as the unfructified Law,
The terrible tentacular rigidity
Of the scorpion and the crab.
As explicit as the adder and the bat-faced jackal
It flattens its unreflective discipline,
Exacts its will.

And all the chuckholes
Back down the road to Jerusalem,

Tremble in the righteous
Outrage of the sun,
The light-drunken Lord,
Horrified of sin,
Dancing his meridianal
Dance of death,
Down toward darkness,
The rain-wreathed regions of the vaster West,
And the salt suck-down of the sea . . .

It is done. Already the desert
Merges its sweeping affirmation,
Redisposing its deft propinquity,
Counting all interruptions
As accidental as birth and as irrelevant as death.
For all its sovereign imperative
The instant must die.
Even the stallion, shock-stung,
Who, pitching that rider down in the dust,
Roached up and ran, even he
Will only a little longer keep,
Etched on the creases of his brain,
The solar-drenched image that flung him so,
Galvanic, pawing the air,
His shrieked nostrils and his socket-sprung jaw,
Tooth-champing, the girth-bursted saddle
Shook free and flung far,
When he leaped loose, and flank-cowering
Ran like a pelted cat,
Bolted for life like some stoned cur,
To meet his death—even he,
Who etched the graph of its sharp kinetic
On his fine-wrought nerve,
Will not hold it long.

That furious light,
More piercing than the atom's

Convulsive flex, and more terrible
Than the star's expiring orgasm,
Will not subsist in his hollow skull
After he dies, thirst-famished,
Out there under those desert cliffs,
Perched upon by those teetering,
Wind-spermed birds, come balancing down,
Leg-light, on the relinquished carcass,
To pick the eyeball expertly out,
Snake forth the brain,
Gobble the entrail and the succulent gut.
Given the desert's immemorial erasures,
Its bone-clean effacements,
This light will die.

But he who bridled that stallion up
And recklessly spurred him,
Who himself lies now like one murderously mauled,
Flat on a bed in the walled town,
Lugging his slow breath,
The stiff-engined heart
Laboring in the shaken ribs,
In him it subsists,
As carefully seeded as some night-borne coal,
Braved through blizzards to a stone-cold hearth,
Where, breathed into life,
Its ray will kindle a glory up,
Warm a world . . .

Before he dies this lapsing,
Shut-tongued wretch
Will spend that vision on the world's width,
Spell utterly out the supreme implication,
Divest his soul of all that was dealt him,
There in the dust, when he lay listening,
His stupefied mind expanding about that central core,
Grasping its depth of total containment,

Its limitless scope. Blind in his bed,
The stony visage, glacial as the implacable rockfaces
That stare east up to Everest,
Thaws in the flow of an understanding.
Peaceful, touched and atoned,
He sinks into sleep. And the scale
Flakes from his eyes.

THE LAST CRUSADE

And how else, she might say, having done it,
Could it ever have happened,
Being all that she was, and he
What he was, and the moment, the time so given,
Almost as meant, and everything
Just as it was,
As it did happen, and all . . .

Climbing the turret in the leasing dawn,
Climbing to taste of the freshness,
To see under her eyes the whole world waken,
Climbing to feel sung into life
Her young skin stippled with coolness,
Climbing the solitary tower,
Risen restless out of that desolated bed,
Sheer orient silk floating, knee and heel outdancing,
Nightgown spanking the flash of her deft shins, the twinkling ankles,
Her limbs a flashing loveliness she knew it,
And none to see the recklessness of racing;
Climbing to savour the taste of the world,
That life, the savour of joy,
In the joy-borne morning.

Bursting into the turret-top chamber
Checked suddenly that way, panting, finding him there,
Prone, all unsuspecting, so fast asleep,
His head thrown back, clear-set curly on the tense pillow,
The boyish face so true to itself in its deep repose and so arresting,
Tower of Eros sprung from the blanket,
Boy and man, so was he, the bulked male body, flowed marble,
All innocent asleep.

How else?

For far on the fields

The somnolent warm and life-bequeathing dawn
Stole in on the world,
Out of the East, coaxing the sibilant shoreline,
Fawning the dulcet wave, the dancing mincing water,
That Mediterranean surge where gods had engendered,
Fertile the womb, cradle of poetry, of song,
Spilth-haunted chambers of the mind's wonder;
That sea and that dawn, they washed the world.

And the small rivers south-bearing,
Winding down to the mother-water,
Thickly ateem, pike-ploughed, the steelhead stinging channel,
Sea-grown hungers seeking their time-lost hatching beds,
The gilt-gravelled shallows, their seed to spawn,
As the long sun spends its final ray when the day declines,
Flecked gold in the shadow.

And under the orchard the ravenous root questing down through the
      glebe
Probing the limestone slab below for the crevice-crack,
That cranny to pierce, to drink up the future through its narrow slit.

And those vineyards, the chequered kingdom, the peasant's realm
      and the Duke's holding,
All his, what is his is hers, is mine, mine to possess, to keep the
      glory—
Those vines lying now in the spring so filmy green with new leaf the
      wakening wind itself risks roughing,
Or how can even the soft of the sun not blister such faintness?
But wine will come at the sap-setting.

And everywhere bird-life, bird-life, those flocked blackbirds and the
      robber jays,
The clatter and call of the north-driven robins,
All the onpressing unstayable migrations,
Up out of Egypt, the tall storks drifting back to the chimney roosts,
All lovemaker birds ablaze, zig-zagging, slitting the sky in scissor-

slashes,
Male to the female feather back blazing, drawn back to the breed,
      sex-song,
For all nature is that, it booms its need, as the male needs the female,
      she is his whole song,
As the birds everywhere, thickset in the lingering reluctant mists,
Tumultuous in the road-flanking thickets, birdsong,
One riotous energizing voice,
A vast jubilation . . .

How else? How else?

For there was her lord the Duke but the Duke was ahunting;
There was the crucifix violent on the wall but the crucifix was stone;
There was conscience, to be sure, conscience, that ragged claw bitten
      between her breasts,
But her breasts burned, so fretful, their ruddy thrust and nuzzle,
Pinking sheer silk, intense, she knew it, dangerous,
But the blood blind, apound, dangerous, all up, and she loved it,
Pausing, watching, her breath slowing down from the tall climb,
Her hand on her breast, the merest brush
Of her own hand on their tingling tips . . .

How else? How else?
Lady and knight, the fine chivalric myth,
In the wakening of the world?

And the door to close.
And the rusty bolt
Shut-set in the dry socket;
That room to cross,
That short floor to travel.
Entranced and alight
She hovered above the slumbrous brow,
The loose-clasped silk,
Burdened within,
All ripeness ajostle—

And felt under her hem
Utterly beyond the reach of her dare
That rude male hand updriven
Gulfing between her laxed legs.

And the spun world downfalling
She slumped, was pulled slotted across,
The torso suddenly flushed
Heat-glutted, the freed fire
Lapped in her loins,
Fiend tongued her,
His paws prowling,
Raged raw fire.

And they paired, whirling,
The stark animal postures,
Fork to fork,
Blunt maleflesh, the spasmed shaft
Retched in her body's croft,
Spewed wrath.

Tongue and maw.
Shocked she saw it.
Thus the mad beasts.

What is sin?

They sprawled apart, flexed.
Crawling back panting he plunged brutally his mouth
Hurting her. Inploughing
The blunt warhead
Chafed like rope-burn.

Ah, what hatred you brute, you brute!

And you slept so still!

Mulling mouth to mouth she matched him.
Is it meat you want, wolf-grinner?

Clenching, she seized the manflesh
Violent, the matted root,
Brought body back,
Bellied against him, splayed,
Snakelike wagging her heavy hips.

Then choke on this!

Back down on the bed,
Her legs asquat,
She thrust it at him,
The hair-clotted hole.

What is sin?
Ha! Pure murder! Then kill
Him with it! Kill
Him . . .!

He reared, the stallion-man,
His head neighing the sky,
The flared nostrils, frightful
His sex the red ruiner, monstrous,
Ran at her.

Don't do that!

Bulge-eyed, mouth maiming wounds on her,
The jabbing eyes,
He crashed across her.
Fright jellied her brain.

What . . . those tearing teeth

My God! . . . huge hands
Split her, the raw crotch
Gaped, maleflesh fierced at her,
That lance he had dreadfully pledged
To kill infidels and beasts . . .

Raging, he ran her up.
She shrieked.

All infidel and beast
She screamed, clawing, the skewered cat.

As the female fights.
As the she-snake toils her prey.
As the she-lion claws the bulked head down of the trampling bull, the
      goring horn.
As the she-beast . . .

She got somehow her nails
Into his face, stiff-fingered
Trenched his streaming cheek,
The claw-gouged eyes.
Her legs sawed the air.
Blue fire burned seething.

Head back, her long hair
Raging round her fighting arms,
Heart roaring the loud demonic yell
She rode him over.

All ache, he struggled her up,
Laboring to free himself,
Rearing up out of eons of slime
His tortured face
Stretched in the mechanistic fury.
A man in a nightmare fighting a snake
He balled her painfully up,

Woman-knot, a frenzied hunk,
Squeezed on that final
Agonizing inch,
One concentrated gout.

Matched, they hung there,
Sustained on the torrent of violation,
The paired wings of terror and lust.

She sang out, triumphant,
Her lips writhing round her teeth,
Chanting, the ultimate
Exultant gloat:

Fuck!

Supreme, the lifted
Evocative animality of her lips,
Floating, the dazed
Illusion of life,
Unspeakable affirmation,
The womb's black finality.

She lifted savagely her face,
Transfixed, the mystery of violation.

The lewd syllable
Sustained in that absolute dimension,
Her body rejoicing on its wound,
Fluted on the primordial memory,
The holocaust of defiance.

All the daughters of Eve
Stamped and twisted,
Swinging the orgiastic strut,
Inducing the final insuperable subjugation:
The phallus of God.

More than virtue,
More than delight,
More than the intellect's
Conceivable beatitude,
The terrible consuming splendor
Of archetypal sin.

Stripped, the blaze of its actuality
Sheathing them round,
Father and daughter
At last confront.

Bound in the primordial equation,
The analogue of all desire,
The secret bond that set them
Hankering down the ages,
Delivered them now
On the matrix of existence,
Each to the other.

From the brain's deep mystery,
From the heart's black hole,
From the pit beyond delusion,
They stared, they knew.

And she broke, terrified,
Sheared sideways,
Doom-spun, spitted on bone,
The fell lance gutting.

No escape, flight forked out of her,
Beaten under the boring horn,
Devil-grasped, she split.
To the death! She keened it, lunging.
Doom gulped at her.
Kill! Bashed down, spiked,

The frame crashing,
Slewed sideways, spasm-sucked.
I die! The fiend firked.
God! Her heart howked it out.
Christ!

Death gobbled her down.

                    *

They lay for a time
Under its brooding prophecy,
Their souls disengaging out of the crucified flesh,
Standing mutely apart,
Watching each other with awe-shamed eyes,
Dumbly regarding the fitful limbs
Unclasping on the bed.

Far off in the world
The vast cities, unclotting,
Released from the torpor of sensual gravitation,
Slowly awoke.

One by one the dazed nerves
Neglected to scream.
The terrified violations
Vanished away.
In a little while
The peace that hushes,
The peace that heals,
Would come home to the lips,
To the eyes.

                    *

He stood suddenly up
His shut face changing,

The coverlet draping his loins as he lifted,
Clinging his frame,
A torn toga.

He stood free of the bed in his short shirt,
The powerful limbs cold-setting,
The sunken sex going soft,
But the face hardening.

He hid his sex with his hand.

Herself, exposed in his act of sudden rising,
The clear body unstirring,
The whole quietude of a passion stanched,
Her arms over her head
She lay with the gown
Clouted above the breasts,
And the breasts unconscious.
But when his glance condemned her
She pulled it,
The sudden guilt to the knees downflexing.

She hid herself from his eyes.

So? her look chided him.
The Beast-Fight done is there nothing more?
We have sinned God knows, but no one else does.
When honor is gone there is yet love.

There is always love.

Her arms lay by her side
Where his guilt had dropped them,
The elbows in,
The forearms trending across her waist,
Hands loose on her thighs,
Laxed either side her body's base,

His passion's pit.

She smiled.
The wan smile of the self-betrayed.
The pain of that plunder
Throbbing the bruise of violation.
She lay, the raped seducer,
Her eyes looking out of innocent untouched deeps,
Her sin blazing there on her bruised forehead,
The crossed brand.

She opened her lips to say
Forgive me
But his face fisted her.

God knows indeed his eyes glared
And so do we.
What did you do it for you bitch
Catch me like this in my friend's castle,
The venerable Duke, and you
The pale Duchess,
My blood lax in sleep,
My reason weak,
Come into this room
Wafting your smooth silk
Pollute my flesh!

He wiped off her slime with a terrible hand.

I took the high vow at Fanjeaux never to rest
Till the fiend was thrown from the Holy Place
And now this.

He turned to dress,
The abrupt movement of pure revulsion.

One course is left me he gritted

To quit the house I have dishonored
And then do penance.

She lay on the bed
Her eyes like a fawn's
Great listening pools of unperplexed silence,
Gazing out of a measureless regard,
Subsumed in the complex infinity of serene comprehension,
The clear morning light falling slantwise across her peaceful body,
The small sounds of morning rising out of the courtyard below,
The far inert fields lying placid beyond the broken moat,
Stretching away to the folded hills and the hushed world beyond.

She opened her lips to say Go then,
A syllable utterly without rancour or condemnation,
Transparently feminine in its unreflecting acceptance of him and of
    her,
The deed, the castle,
The moment and the world,
The last crusade,
Contained in them and containing them,
At peace, the winey ardour
Quelled in her loins,
Instinct with seed . . .

But on that instant
Hell froze, and the Duke's men
Bashed in the door.

IN SAVAGE WASTES

A monk ran into a party of handmaids of the Lord on a certain journey. Seeing them he left the road and gave them a wide berth. But the Abbess said to him: If you were a perfect monk, you would not even have looked close enough to see that we were women.

—VERBA SENIORUM

A hermit who has lived a long time in the desert experiences great dearth of spirit, and one night, exhausted, falls asleep over his prayers. He is awakened by a knock at the door, and opening it beholds two nuns. They explain that they are on pilgrimage and have become separated from their company, and beg of him shelter for the night. He graciously shows them into his cell, and prepares to spend the night outside so that they may have its privacy to themselves. However, once inside they lock the door and throwing off their habits reveal themselves as naked succubi. They cast a spell over him, and seduce him, and there is not a shred of sensory excitation which they do not stimulate within him and gratify.

In the morning the monk wakes up and realizes he has dreamed. There is no sign either of pilgrims or succubi, nor any evidence of the disorders so real to him during the night. The monk leaves his desert cell and begins to make his way back to the world. As he goes he meets a young man, vaguely familiar to him, who is newly dressed in a monk's habit and is entering the desert to become a solitary. The young monk seems to recognize him and calls him by name; kneeling before him he asks his blessing. Then he says to him: "Tell me, Father, what is the greatest blessing and the greatest curse of the spiritual life?" The monk replies: "Sleep. In sleep we dream. In dreams we betray ourselves. In betrayal we discover ourselves. In self-discovery we lose our innocence. In loss of innocence we gain knowledge. In knowledge we gain wisdom. In wisdom we recover innocence. God be with you." With these words the monk leaves the young man, whom he now recognizes as himself, and re-enters the world.

I too, O God, as You very well know,
Am guilty.

And the desert gorges, those hacked
Untendered waste-worlds of the soul—
What buzzard's eye from its sun-skewered height
Has peered such places,
Pierced such deeps?

The gullies of death, the engorged
Arroyos, badlands of the hackling heart,
The scups of perversity.

I too, I too, as You very well know . . .

Where the kites are shrieking
There reeks the carcass.
Where the treasure is sunk
There cowers the heart.
Having done such things in the green wood
What will I do in the dry?

Guilt-stretched the night.
Choked in the abstract dimension
I see the eyes of my lust.

Have pity on me, have pity on me,
At least you my friends,
For God hath touched me.

For the light is lost.
Great darknesses drop over the waste.
The hostile stars burn green as cat's eyes
In their depth of dread.
There is not an owl on the greasewood,
There is not a saw-whet on the creosote bush
To keep a man company.

I too, O God, as You very well know,
Am guilty.

For I sought and found not,
I searched, but was not successful.
When I failed, You drew back the veil,
And I am in terror.

In terror,
Who gazed in the poisonous pool.
In dread,
Who sucked of its jet.
Am sick and am sick
Who have seen to myself,
Begging forgiveness of my own self,
In what I have done.

For if You, O God, can pardon a man,
Should himself be less merciful?

Let me forgive myself of my terrible sins
That I may have peace.

Let me have mercy on myself
Or I will hang myself on a juniper tree
To wipe out my guilt.

There will be flints and grits forever in my bed.
There will be cinders in my mush.

I am burned black.
I am back from a bitter journey.
I have cruised hell.

Let me forgive myself
That thought to be a saint

And am proved a monster.
That thought to be righteous and good,
And am proved vile.
That thought myself to be the Christ
And am found the Devil.

Windless, the air dead, the night hot.
Can I find, in fact, the friendliness of a human face?

Forgive me, O God, that my heart should hold such horrors.

The vast desert stars.
The waterless ridges.
The vacant gullies.

When I am proved out
I will come back to my people
And confess my crimes.

For I will make friends of the sinner
And comfort him in his plight.
I will pick the evildoer up from the ground
That he may take heart from his evil
And hunger the good.

I will bless the bad,
That he may be brought from madness,
May be made whole.

Speechless the stars.
No word in the wind.
The hell of nature defiled
Shuts her dread face.

For there is no man that is righteous
But carries somewhere in his salty heart
A worse villainy.

Never a man without his vices.
If any man doubts it
He has not sunk to the whoredom of his heart,
Nor tongued his own flesh.

Our loves betray us.
We give ourselves to God
And in our faithlessness
Play strumpet to the Devil.

Thus it is that my hate is scribbled about my mouth
And my lust rings my eyes.

My guilt is blistered upon my hands.
They have prized blood.
They are dabbed with sin.

O my God, my God, what can I say
Except that Thou hast touched me?

In sleep, in deep slumber,
In the raw desert night,
Thou didst sent Thy holy devils
There to accost me.
As Thy terrible henchmen
They did show me me.

What visions of vastness on the moon-sunken wastes?
So dry is the night the dust-devils wander,
They whisper me out.

I will go back once more to the city of man,
Will abase myself before the sinner
For he is cleaner than I.

At least he never has claimed to be good,

Nor supposed himself righteous.

At least he does not swear by Thy truth
And live by his lies.

At least he does not bless with the one hand
While he horribly defiles with the other.

Forgive me, dear Christ, and make me as Thyself,
Who knew Thy true Self.

Hot night. The crude desert stars. The devouring distances.
There is not a coyote's howl to quaver the darkness.
There is not the scuttle of a deermouse nor the slow drag of a serpent.
There is not the mutter of a single leaf
So heavy hangs the air.

O my soul, my soul, what deaths, what pits, what savageries, what
          wastes!

If I could touch so much as a piece of human dung
That some hapless wanderer dropped by a yucca
I should consider myself not friendless.

But my thoughts return upon me
And I dare not sleep,
For I am in dread of my dreams.

Therefore in the morning will I go forth
And return to the ways of man.

I will seek God henceforth in the shameful human face.
I will serve God in the wretched human act.
I will savour God in the salt of human tears.

In the body's corruptness will He be revealed to me,
In the postures of defloration,

In the deeds of wrath.

Where the murderer strangles his hope,
Where the thief plunders his heart,
Where the ogler gloats and gloats on his own self
And gloating profanes.

Out of these, out of these, will Thy peace shine forth
If I show pity.

No day? No dawn? No water? No wet?
A drop of grace for my parched tongue,
One drop would suffice me.

Forgive me, that my heart was vicious.
In my viciousness of heart
I coupled the bitch.

But in the spate of such hardness
Thou didst come to redeem me.
Hadst Thou not discovered my sin to myself
Thou couldst never have touched me to forgive me.
Therefore blessed is my sin.

I will seek out a human face that I may know pity.
That I might betray and be forgiven.
That I might be betrayed and forgive.

I will seek love in the face of a man
And pity in the eyes of a woman.

I will seek faith in the brow of a child.

I will return to my mother,
To the breasts of her that nursed me,
To the lap of her that bore me.

And I will find my father.
He will bless my head.
He will forgive me.

Therefore will I be whole again,
And be made new again,
And again be made as a child.

For the night is dark.
But off in the east I see low light.
I smell the dawn.

And will find my God in the thwarted love that breaks between us!

BOOK FIVE:
EROS & THANATOS
1962

THE POET IS DEAD

A MEMORIAL FOR ROBINSON JEFFERS

*To be read with a full stop between the strophes,
as in a dirge.*

In the evening the dusk
Stipples with lights. The long shore
Gathers darkness in on itself
And goes cold. From the lap of silence
All the tide-crest's pivotal immensity
Lifts into the land.

*

Snow on the headland,
Rare on the coast of California.
Snow on Point Lobos,
Falling all night,
Filling the creeks and the back country,
The strangely beautiful
Setting of death.

*

For the poet is dead.
The pen, splintered on the sheer
Excesses of vision, unfingered, falls.
The heart-crookt hand, cold as a stone,
Lets it go down.

*

The great tongue is dried.
The teeth that bit to the bitterness
Are sheathed in truth.

If you listen
You can hear the field mice
Kick little rifts in the snow-swirls.
You can hear
Time take back its own.

*

For the poet is dead.
On the bed by the window,
Where dislike and desire
Killed each other in the crystalline interest,
What remains alone lets go of its light. It has found
Finalness. It has touched what it craved: the passionate
Darks of deliverance.

*

At sundown the sea wind,
Burgeoning,
Bled the west empty.

*

Now the opulent
Treacherous woman called Life
Forsakes her claim. Blond and a harlot
She once drank joy from his narrow loins.
She broke his virtue in her knees.

*

In the water-gnawn coves of Point Lobos
The white-faced sea otters

Fold their paws on their velvet breasts
And list waveward.

*

But he healed his pain on the wisdom of stone.
He touched roots for his peace.

*

For the poet is dead. The gaunt wolf
Crawled out to the edge and died snapping.
He said he would. The wolf
Who lost his mate. He said he would carry the wound,
The blood-wound of life, to the broken edge
And die grinning.

*

Over the salt marsh the killdeer,
Unrestrainable,
Cry fear against moonset.

*

And all the hardly suspected
Latencies of disintegration
Inch forward. The skin
Flakes loss. On the death-gripped feet
The toenails glint like eyeteeth
From the pinched flesh.
The caged ribs and the bladed shoulders,
Ancient slopes of containment,
Imperceptibly define the shelves of structure,
Faced like rock ridges
Boned out of mountains, absently revealed
With the going of the snow.

*

In the sleeve of darkness the gopher
Tunnels the sod for short grass
And pockets his fill.

*

And the great phallus shrinks in the groin,
The seed in the scrotum
Chills.

*

When the dawn comes in again,
Thoughtlessly,
The sea birds will mew by the window.

*

For the poet is dead. Beyond the courtyard
The ocean at full tide hunches its bulk.
Groping among the out-thrusts of granite
It moans and whimpers. In the phosphorescent
Restlessness it chunks deceptively,
Wagging its torn appendages, dipping and rinsing
Its ripped sea rags, its strip-weeded kelp.
The old mother grieves her deathling.
She trundles the dark for her lost child.
She hunts her son.

*

On the top of the tower
The hawk will not perch tomorrow.

But in the gorged rivermouth
Already the steelhead fight for entry.
They feel fresh water
Sting through the sieves of their salt-coarsened gills.
They shudder and thrust.

So the sea broods. And the aged gull,
Asleep on the water, too stiff to feed,
Spins in a side-rip crossing the surf
And drags down.

This mouth is shut. I say
The mouth is clamped cold.
I tell you this tongue is dried.

But the skull, the skull,
The perfect sculpture of bone!—
Around the forehead the fine hair,
Composed to the severest
Lineaments of thought,
Is moulded on peace.

And the strongly-wrought features,
That keep in the soul's serenest achievement
The spirit's virtue,
Set the death mask of all mortality,
The impress of that grace.

*

In the shoal-champed breakers
One wing of the gull
Tilts like a fin through the ribbon of spume
And knifes under.

*

And all about there the vastness of night
Affirms its sovereignty. There's not a cliff
Of the coastline, not a reef
Of the waterways, from the sword-thrust Aleutians
To the scorpion-tailed stinger Cape Horn—
All that staggering declivity
Grasped in the visionary mind and established—
But is sunken under the dark ordainment,
Like a sleeper possessed, like a man
Gone under, like a powerful swimmer
Plunged in a womb-death washed out to sea
And worked back ashore.

*

The gull's eye,
Skinned to the wave, retains the ocean's
Imponderable compression,
And burns yellow.

*

The poet is dead. I tell you
The nostrils are narrowed. I say again and again
The strong tongue is broken.

*

But the owl
Quirks in the cypresses, and you hear
What he says. He is calling for something.
He tucks his head for his mate's
Immemorial whisper. In her answering voice
He tastes the grace-note of his reprieve.

*

When fog comes again to the canyons
The redwoods will know what it means.
The giant sisters
Gather it into their merciful arms
And stroke silence.

*

You smell pine resin laced in the salt
And know the dawn wind has veered.

*

And on the shelf in the gloom,
Blended together, the tall books emerge,
All of a piece. Transparent as membranes
The thin leaves of paper hug their dark thoughts.
They know what he said.

*

The sea, reaching for life,
Spits up the gull. He falls spread-eagled,
The streaked wings swept on the sand.
Vague fingers of snow, aimlessly deft, grope for his eyes.
When the blind head snaps
The beak krakes at the sky.

*

Now the night closes.
All the dark's negatory
Decentralization
Quivers toward dawn.

*

He has gone into death like a stone thrown in the sea.

*

And in far places the morning
Shrills its episodes of triviality and vice
And one man's passing. Could the ears
That hardly listened in life
Care much less now?

*

Snow on the headland,
The strangely beautiful
Oblique concurrence,
The strangely beautiful
Setting of death.

*

The great tongue
Dries in the mouth. I told you.
The voiceless throat
Cools silence. And the sea-granite eyes.
Washed in the sibilant waters
The stretched lips kiss peace.

*

The poet is dead.

*

Nor will ever again hear the sea lions
Grunt in the kelp at Point Lobos.
Nor look to the south when the grunion
Run the Pacific, and the plunging
Shearwaters, insatiable,
Stun themselves in the sea.

MISSA DEFUNCTORUM

The preacher's coagulated rhetoric
Evaporates in his teeth, unretainable. The shiver of bells
And the narcotic pungence of burnt incense
Dissolve in the sheer exhaustion of time,
And the long rite closes. Holy water
Slashes right and left across the snouted coffin,
Malignant as a crocodile, glaring balefully out
Through the barricaded portal, ready to rush.
Then the cantors arise, bowing, turning,
Intoning somberly the thudded
Inflections of the *De Profundis,*
And we front the door. Lifting our eyes
We see the laity lurch to their feet, the slogged faces
Insensible between death's radical incomprehensibility
And the pulverization of empacted Latin.
The coffin scuttles through, bloated with prey, menacing.
Immobilized on the apex of a congealed terror
We grip the pews, and pray deliverance.

And like something desperately brought back to life
We stagger through to clear air. A taut Sicilian
Breaks from the crowd, makes toward the insolent red convertible
Toothing the curb, all white-wall tires and a rash of chrome.
He halfway slithers behind the wheel, is reaching for the ignition
When I spot the wife: spike-heeled, snug-waisted, her skirt
Glued to her hip, the bosom
Bare under black tulle, but the eyes hunted,
The hair toppling like a wave, and on the proud stunned features
The mouth blunt as a wound. She wrenches the handle and crawls in,
Her shoulders sagged, all the pouting provocation
Of the breast's aggressive petulance
Collapsed in the slump of contained exhaustion.
But the long legs go scissoring in, and the oblique skirt,
Hitched giddily clear, bludgeons the friars
With a cut of naked thigh. She hauls in her feet

And the door pounds. I see her lips
Writhe on the root of a cigarette: "For God's sake Tony
G'me a light. Let's
Get the hell out of here!" And the clutch
Grabs.

      And my heart
Slams on the impact of all carnality,
Its cry of survival, the plunge back to life.
What detonations of suppressed ferocity
Crackling under the glazed surfaces!
What spurts of aggression
Erupting out of the pent ventricles!
The friars pace by: *A portae inferi*
Erue Domine animas eorum! But the red convertible
Is gone, tearing a gash through reality
More violent than the purifying apogees of pain
And more terrible, roaring back down the loud arterials
To the gaped heart's hole,
Where the vulva and the cod,
Clutched in the blood's
Devouring paroxysm,
Beat back death.

MISSA SANCTORUM

The sensuality of women at Mass: that deceptive
Complaisance, coming ardently alert
To adore, to kneel in finery, displaying the erotic foot,
The deft ankle and the shapely leg, sleek in sheer hose.

All down the centuries the preachers have thundered,
Denouncing over and over: "Have you no shame!"
Rebuking the sensual insolence, the crimson
Lips and the kohl-darkened eyes,
But to no avail, and now no more.
Awash on the back-roil of the world
They have given it up. The women have won.

And come with their heads bent and their haunches trembling,
The snug waist tucked in close to the table of the Lord,
As in love, knees slackly apart, but the stern
Taut, expectant, tightening for the faintest
Suggestible pelvic thrust when the head
Lifts up and goes back to receive
God. And the swan-like throat a marble fluting,
A stem of ivory for the chalice of the lips.

Oh, more svelte than Ashtoreth and her temple harlots
The Christian women, chaste yet complicit
(Else why would they do this?) bring the simmering flesh
To offer it up.

　　　　　And behind them their men,
Withdrawn in the ineluctable isolation of Adam,
Gaze out of the eyes of an abstract remoteness, uncomprehending,
While their wives and their daughters
Prostrate the flesh.

　　　　　As when Eva and Ave,
The pride and the presence,

Disengenuously meek, a kind of awesome
Virginal guile, brought the heart of man
And the hunger of God
To heel.

BOOK SIX:
THE ROSE OF SOLITUDE
1960-1966

PROLOGUE

The dark roots of the rose cry in my heart.
They pierce through rock-ribs of my stony flesh,
Invest the element, the loam of life,
They twist and mesh.

The red blood of the rose beats on, beats on,
Of passion poured, of fiery love composed,
Virtue redeemed, the singular crest of life,
And pride deposed.

Love cries regenerate and lust moans consumed,
Shaken in terror on that rage of breath.
Untrammeled still the red rose burns on
And knows no death.

Petal by crimson petal, leaf by leaf,
Unfolds the luminous core, the bright abyss,
Proffers at last the exquisite delight
Of the long kiss.

Until shall pass away the wasted means
Leaving in essence what time held congealed:
The Sign of God evoked from the splendid flesh
Of the Rose revealed.

PART ONE: I NAIL MY LIFE

THE WAY OF LIFE AND THE WAY OF DEATH

I

Mexico: and a wind on the mesa
Blowing its way out of sluggish centers,
Coaxing a tropical fragrance,
The moist rains of December.

Mangoes and rum, the bright
Blades of poinsettias.

A soft call of birds in the forest,
A sound of women dipping water at wells,
The taunting of little children.

I think of poinsettias out of the earth,
Red as a rose in the teeth of a woman,
Black as the hair of the Virgin of Guadalupe,
As shaken with passion as the spilled Blood of Christ.

I split my heart on the blood of Mexico.
I have nailed myself to the Mexican cross.

II

I have nailed myself to the Mexican cross,
The flint knife of her beauty.

I hunger the solace of mango fruit,
The woman-flesh of the guava.

Desire splits on the quick of poinsettias,
Stung to the rake of Mexican nettle.

262

I am shambled in trees,
Thirsting the riverstone of God,
The waterwells of passion.

Her limbs! Her limbs! the witchery of her excellent legs!
The Mexican glimmer along the lips!
The clicking teeth of her laughter!

Nailed. Split. Crucified. Scourged.

Shrieked on the cross,
Flayed to the slump of the devastated heart,
My body blazes.

III

My body blazes.
In the pound of blood all meaning moves,
All movement dazes.

She flashes her eyes.
Mexico shudders under the leaves,
Shaking the branches.

In the lithe ripple of whispering feet,
In the clear spurt of laughter.

In the high peal of rivering lips,
The stunned lurch of passion.

I am agonized on the Mexican cross
In the hopeless fashion.

I cry. I cry.

Will she burn me out,
Char the body ashen?

Let the white hope live,
Make the black hope die.

I suffer the lance-thrust under the rib:
One pierce of her eye.

IV

I suffer the lance.
I faint on the sexual cross
Of this Mexican madness.

I am fierced. My flesh is stitched
With a riddle of lips.

On the blade of the crimson poinsettia
She has gashed my side.

With one wound of her lips,
With one of the little wantonnesses
She works with her fingers.

The flesh of the mango fruit!
The ravishing meat of the guava!

Why must God deny me?

Where is my boast?
What has come of my strife?

On the Mexican cross,
Between the two thieves of her eyes,

I nail my life.

I nail my life.

Am laid in the tomb of immolation.

Wrapped in silence,
Packed about with aloes and spices,
Her pledge suffices.

I rest in rock.

Hidden behind a slab of stone,
Shielded and safe from the curse of soldiers.

I await her word,
The syllable of grave inflection,
Salving the sting of crimson poinsettias,
Healing the wound of the Mexican cross.

I dream the dawn of the longest night:
The one resurrection.

THE KISS OF THE CROSS

I cry.

Once of this world,
Woman of God,
What do you betoken?

Heart of fire,
Violence of flesh,
The spirit's flash,
Voice of tolled desire.

Tongue of wrath,
Latencies, the fierce
Evocation: semblances,
The shut darkness broken.

Over the bay
City-light wavers and spurns.
One steamer
Sidles the mist,
Homes the black harbor.

Pound heart,
Heart of the splendored rapture,
Ruptured on death.

In the trace of a hand,
On the mystery of a face
The brute heart is shaken.

II

The heart reaves: my flesh
Coughs from its clotted need,
One flex of possession.

All flung pride
Crashes on that crest.

Her face reels,
God's voice blares.

The crucifix
Snaps.

In the tongs of passion
Is torn,
Is torn.

Let the heart be hit
If ever it can.
Let the bludgeoned soul
Stone its mute mouth.

In the outreach of love,
In the passion of possession,
I nailed my desire.

III

Heart be hushed.
Let it howk and then hush.

Let the black wave break.
Let the terrible tongue
Engorge my deeps.

Let the loins of ferocity
Lave my shut flesh.

I killed the Christ.

On the inch of my pride,
On the diamond of my desire,
In the pierce of a woman's goodness,
By the token of her grace.

I who crept toward him year after year
Murdered my God.

IV

I crept.

I brought Him gifts,
Hushed in my heart.

I brought what I had.

I crept.

I gave Him every gift of myself.
I brought Him all the wholeness I had.

V

I brought Him my wholeness,
That wholeness was split.

I brought Him my burden,
That burden broke.

I brought Him my all,
My all was empty.

In the wrath of flesh
I heard His bone
Snap like a nerve.

My passion poured.

VI

My passion poured.

I heard His nerve
Snap like a bone.

I came:
    up out of darkness,
    deep holes and recesses,
    black wells and cisterns of the self—
I came!
I came!

I cried my pang!
The burden
Split bone in the dark!

He shrieked.

As I gasped
He fell dead.

I panted across her face
Feeling Him bleed.

I saw her kneel.
She kissed His cross.

VII

She kissed.
My shame charred my face.
With her voice she consoled.
In her mother-hands
She knitted His bones.

When she kissed His knees
His face smiled.

I thrashed in that dark
Strangled with guilt.

What deeds of wrath from the spilt gift!

Shameful the face of the shocked man
Who wept in my place.

I spit heart's blood.
My fist a claw
Scrabbled my heart.

She kissed.
I saw Him sag.

That dark was dead.

VIII

She kissed.

With her lips she consoled.
My soul shook.

I screeched back in dread.

As a cool water flows
Her words were.

I saw stars steeped in death over San Francisco.

Her words:
She gave up a song that a heart might heal.
I flinched on her prayer.

Picking my sin like a stone out of dirt
I bore it home.

I held it against my raddled groin,
My jewel of pain on which Christ died.

While I slept it burned on.

IX

While I slept it burned.
A stone in my bed it lay nightlong,
A passion to purge me.

In my mirror of death
Her face sustained me.

271

In my substance of guilt
Her purity betrayed me.

I slashed with my seed.

She bore the flesh-wound under the breast,
The mother-burden.

By the kissed cross,
Where the Christ-nerve
Snapped when my passion poured,
Clinched on the Tree:

She brought me back.

x

She brought me back.
The kiss that kept me:

A heart to heal,
A death to die,
The debt of a death.

I was brought back alive.

Drenched in that deed when passion poured,
Her purity betrayed me.

Merciless that armor
Turned the point of my brutal tongue.

I fell stunned.

She picked up the pieces.
One by one she put them together.
Piece by piece she made a whole.

She brought back a man.

XI

Cross-kissed I stagger.

Her face that broke the harbor's beauty
Revokes my passion.

A graciousness redeems.

In the purity of touch,
On the trace of a selfless passion,

Athwart the trajectory of an ancient lust,
I signed a saint.

Her lips, her lips, the mystery of a perfect face!

She bowed her head when Christ broke.
As I wept she smiled.

In the innocence of little children
Her wisdom wells:

My choked desire.

XII

O Christ & Lady
Save me from my law!

O Christ & Lady
Save me from my seed!

O Christ & Lady
Save me from my tongue!

O Christ & Lady
Save me from my curse!

O Christ & Lady
Save me from my moan!

O Christ & Lady
O Christ & Lady

Save me from myself!

XIII

Let no woe be spoken.

Wake not a word.
No haplessness unearth
From any deepness broken.

A timelessness of pain,
An endlessness of love,
The mystery of person.

Redeemed, restored,
She verifies my token:

God is not gone.

Christ is not cold.
The Wound will not worsen.

IMMORTAL STRANGENESS

I

Spring. And in the vanquishing
Of winter, the song of a bird
All night long over San Francisco,
The southland stranger, his voice
Caroling a cool rapture:
He twirled a dream.

A dream tormented.
A dream betokened.
A dream conceived.

His throat bled. He cried out,
A heart-rip of brutal passion, spirited
And transfigured in the ecstasy of song:
He shuddered a truth.

In the dream his heart bled.
The mind spoke No but his beak
Bled on the mortal wound: his love's
Immortal strangeness.

His voice
Bled on its sob.
He curled tongue.
In the doubt, the chill whisper,
His heart evoked a strange freedom.

Over the No,
Over the No,
The word of the will, his voice
Curled and fluted; his tongue
Cut that Yes.

Cut yes. His voice
Bled. We heard the will
Caught on its No
But the bleeding tongue.

She turned. Her eyes
In that dark, over the chilled
Liquor, the flagrant rum,
Pierced veiled dangers; doubts
Pierced on silences.

I lurched. When her head
Turned, my mouth
Groped. In the clenched
Darkness, the rose unfolding,
The lipped unloosening leaves,
Yield of the crimson heart:
The dream pierced.

Song bled. In the brutal
Heart of the tyrant bird
Conscience, shook on the pierced contraction,
Spurned. Her eyes veiled.
She bent. Let the Holy Ghost,
Hawk of the brutal flesh,
Be blessed by a bird.

III

Be blessed. That bird
Cried out all night,

The southland stranger,
Rare on the roofs of San Francisco.

I heard in my brain
The redoubtable No
But the bird yessed it.

We kissed. I felt birdsong
Blaze in my brain,
The purled pealing.

Her flesh, buckling,
Shuddered under my tilt.

In the rose revealed
The flesh found force,
Spurt of shagged rapture.

Mouth cupped on mouth,
Stunned, on the struck
Song, we clung.

IV

Cried Yes!

I smote the wall
With my balled fist.

She clutched air, emptiness,
A thickness flooding about the knees.

Limb-lash, wrapped,
A hacking ratchet.

We block.

A long twinging lightning
Flickers the loins,
Licks through us,
Slips bristling meshes:

Those lion-nerved noises
The whole need makes when it scents rut,
Snuffs scut in its nostril.

A trampling of footpads
Pummels the flesh,
An ecstasy of thrust.

Lips fight, teeth clash,
Tongue torturing tongue.

v

Now up from down under
The long stitch of manflesh
Goes suckering in.

All that fretfulness
Shucked now,
Purled shuddering under.

It is the make of the male.

An odor of sperm,
Sea-smell, salt,
Waft of all women,
Savor.

And womb: loosed of this longing
Return, return,
Back to beginnings.

Sea-sourced,
A rock jutting,
Toothed in her.

Spray drenched,
Spiced spume on wet beaches,
The bone-chaliced vestry.

Sea-sourced.
Cove-closed.
Wave-washed.

VI

She falls still,
Under my spentness,
Breathing.

I grope across her spoiled pride,
All shattered passion, her virtue
Shambled about my loins,
Nakedly dripping.

Floor cold
Floods us with chill,
Chastens the heat-flushed limbs,
Repents.

In the Rose revealed
The seed shakes free, streaks home,
Wrigs.

She struggles up,
Groping her clothes together,
Pushing, protesting.

When we fell—
    on the hard floor,
    in the harsh dark,
    on the bitter boards—,
When we fell
We rose.

VII

We rose.

She plaited her hair.

Woman of God,
Once of this world,
When a bird cried out over San Francisco,
Was blindness blessed?

Was blessing
Born of a bird's song,
A sin redeemed?

Is sin
Transformed in ecstasy,
In love reprieved?

Can love
Annul a sin's stain,
Can a bird bless a wound?

VIII

Bless a wound?

In the transparent night,
In the spring,
Her lips—

One mockingbird
Threaded the dark with cool delight!

I heard his oath.
I staggered against the presence of God,
I dropped for default.

Somewhere within
Pools of silence drank rifts of semblance
In the swell of time.

Across her brow the song trilled on,
Merging, mocking.

My mind
Struck bars of moonshaft
Filtering doom.

Braced on belief,
Kept there,
A man of remorse,

I could only bless.

IX

Could bless. Cried
The benediction of the bond.

She only smiled.

Her eyes veiled a wisdom.

I cried words of proof.
Is joy the justification,
Justification the joy?

She only smiled. Hush.
Be troubled nothing to speak.
Be still. I was hushed.

Her eyes, the woman-wisdom
Deeper and more meant than the kerns of my man,
Gave no answers up.

Wisdom of the flesh,
Woman's old immutable law,
And the blood oath
Pledged of the past.

A truth to be.

X

A truth to be.

In her term,
That finality,
I dipped and was purged.

Where was the seed that sprang in the night
Lipped in the rose?

She smiled. In her wisdom
She cradled my head.

On her breast's bourn I lay.

Along the line of my brow
Her lips led, her fern breath blessed me.

What had I wrought in her woman's womb,
My man's pride?

She smiled. My hand
Broke to the ground.

Over the roof
The bird bore on,
The torrent-tongue, vocable
Of an infused rapture,
A taunting truth.

Shocked on the inviolable
Empathy, kind keening to kind, our ears
Rang realness.

We believed ourselves blessed.

XI

We believed.

Night fails,
Gropes out to sea,

Questioning.

What seed stirs yet
In the flesh of the rose?

What bird burns the dawn,
Unappeased of his violent blessing?

I hear his rage of brute voracity
Throat his red love.

I hear his madness
Provoke the obdurate shuttage
Round reason's range,
This substance of thrust.

Can a bird absolve?
In the violence of flesh
His mindlessness
Annuls without cease
Explicit reversals,
Brooks the burden back.

Her eyes
Shone wisdom.

She shut my mouth.
She laid a hand on my face.
I cut contradictions.

She smiled
And shone wisdom out of her brow.

I preached
The justice in the joy.

She shut my tongue.

XII

She muted
My mouth.

I say nothing.

In the dawn
She goes down.

In the church she chooses
Kneels now at the cross.

In the closed
Confessional
Bends down and is purged.

I beat my fist on the wall.

Woman of God!
Does not a bird absolve?

She smiled and left me.
She followed
Her thirst's deep truth
To its source
That driven dawn.

I beat my fist.

I heard the bird
Borne out and on of the windowed heart,
A song of reprieve.

XIII

A song. But in the heart's
Red rage I bulk through.

When does a sin
Become its virtue?

I wrest the prongs of my contradiction.
I plague my mind with devils and thorns.
I toss to my angel.

Christ and Master!
On the cross you wept!
Read my blunt heart!

She smiles and says nothing.
In her woman's wisdom
Born of the violated flesh,
Self-seared in a surged
Recklessness of heart,
I sense the saint.

Did a bird absolve?
She smiles and stirs.

Cut on the rose
Reach of contrition
My pride pales.

Her eyes annul me.

Facing their force
I scuttle wrath.
I drop defeated.

XIV

I dropped defeated,
Rose renewed.

And in the cry of a bird
Have seized salvation.

In the sin's red gape
I crawl through;
I seize salvation.

The benediction of a bird
Stabs and transforms.
I seize salvation.

Heartwound of Christ.
Headwound of God.

Above the pang of a bird
The sheer smile of a woman's wisdom,
I touch reprieve.
I seize salvation.

And kneel, crouching and confessing.

Under the stroked
Gesture of absolution
I kneel, plowing
Clots off my greaves,
And swaying stand.

In the breaded sacrament
I eat my God.

In the plunged wine
Tell truth drunk down.

On her lips,
Her lips,
In the *agon* of a bird,
I seize salvation.

The spirit has spoken,
The Spirit speaks.

*

And shredding the east
The blood-bellied sun
Erupts and debouches,
A surge-swelling rush.

Rolled over hills
It throbs and pulses,
All about it fluctuant air
Shivers and breaks.

I see myriads of fleck
Whorl and ascend,
Articulating vast seizures,
Gross instances,
Arpeggios of dream,
Dissonances of raptness,
A vortex of crest.

There is a walking world
About my knees as I pray.

I think moons of kept measure.
I find at my fingers

A seethe of splendor
A surge-up of source.

I sense vast clefts of emptiness
Spoiling for love.

I hear the flux and glut of violent causes.
I taste a distilled harmonic
Beyond the surfaces of trend.

I hear in my deeps
Pealings of horns,
Far trumpets of succinctness,
A blare of band and zithers of light.

I savor moans of brass.
It falls about me in sings of peace,
A treading of feet on the stairs of redress.

Hear me forever in Thy towers of peace
O Lord and my God,
O maker and creator,
Heart within heart,
The long dream of durance.

I press on.
I will not be cozened.
I have evinced finality.
I know clear oath.

Drenched in its depth
The long lesson of the life
Finds its point and hub,
A meaning zoned on tridents of gem,
One garnet of joy.

Speechless, the holiest

Gag of rejoicement
Shutters my tongue.

I eat tempos of change.
Standing, I exult.

My act
Lives blessed.

XV

My act lives.

From its life delivered
I stand free.

Of the Rose renewed
I rise, I rise.
I stand free.

In the wisdom of the flesh,
In the truth of the touch,
In the silence of the smile

Redeemed.

Under the blessing of a bird
I seize freedom.

Traced out of hell,
Through the mystery of love,
In the ecstasy of the Bird,
The Rose revealed:

I stand free.

PART TWO: FIRE IN ICE

THE CANTICLE OF THE ROSE

Because in the deepnesses of night you smoulder a ray that does not violate the dark but solemnly defines it;

Because in the resonance of noon you lease a memory of night that never blemishes the day but gratefully relieves it;

Because in the hesitance of dusk you mirror gloams that do not shiver light from dark but imperceptibly compose them;

I confess thee, and acknowledge thee: in thy mystery of depth I see in all thou art the lambent modes of the divine.

Because in the aftermath of time your being does not crumble with the past but brilliantly conserves it;

Because in the shaping of the future your spirit does not choke eventuality but vibrantly extends it;

Because in the instantaneity of the present your existence does not close reality but irrepressibly expands it;

I confess thee, and acknowledge thee: in thy mystery of depth I hear in all thou art the voiceless harmonies of God.

For what blooms behind your lips moves ever within my sight the kept diffusion of the smile;

And what dawns behind your brow subsists within my thought the somnolent mystery of mind;

And what trembles in your words lives on forever in my heart the immutable innerness of speech;

Therefore do I confess thee, and acknowledge thee: in thy mystery of depth I touch in all thou art the shut profundity of God.

And hear always at night in rivers of sleep the pulsant murmuration of your voice;

Nor do any words you have uttered but pool in my mind, crisping on somehow toward my heart's repository cleft,

Potent with implication, unsearchable with wisdom, the haunting and superlative inflection

292

Of one who holds the token of her own exemplar, possessing that
    preeminence of self, its unselfconscious deftness of response,
Sustaining prescience, an unsurpassable élan of quest, an incontest-
    able justness of perception.

And have cried out in your arms across my lips those words your
    wisdom bore within my sanguinary pain,
And cradled in my heart that nakedness of soul the unblemished
    marvel of your flesh made manifest from wisdom's womb,
And traced along those lips the delineaments of a primordial under-
    standing, modulant of time, the strictures of an irrepressible
    blitheness,
And source of that awareness kept without diminution in every tilt
    and nuance of your unitary being.

Do not believe because I am man and friable love has addled my brain
    so that I speak from daftness only,
Nor ever suppose enchantment feeds exaggeration hoping an induced
    reward might grace my love-starved throat,
Nor discount as the elaborate rhetoric of the poet's practional art an
    indulgent richness of the luxuriant tongue:
I know too well the accents of excess to be deceived by them,
As he who fashions speech knows better by far its procreant liabilities
    than any who listen merely.

(Is it not plain I pile language up to check and impede the rising tide
    within me,
Containing in its plex the mastering flood, conserving the vowel-weft
    over against its consonantal check,
To hold the importunate crest of my elation, that I might touch the
    hidden nerve springing volition free,
And of its concentrated force perfectly specify the fierce insurgent
    reck, the absolute object of my attestation?)

But rather, disposed in whatsoever strategem of bland containment
    instinct might contrive
My art can err only in insufficiency, my fierce excesses crack on the

ineluctable reality of what you are,

Proving, as demonstration ever must prove, the meaning not of your, but my, deficiency,

That anything I utter must emerge but as the pale reflection of your crucial salient truth,

As words forever are mocked by the essential presences of living fact preceding them in being.

Therefore do I speak. I cry out. I rejoice. I exult in the uncontainable triumph of God,

Praising Him in you Who has created you in such profound extremeness of effectuated being,

And stroked in gratitude kneel in the generosity of that solar Christ Who blazed you across my life, searing me with your essence;

And I stagger in the excess of that Spirit Who brimmed you with His fierce charisma,

Expanding utterly beyond your shadowed definition the presage of His overmastering fact.

And celebrate the truth, knowing that in the cloudy exigence of act even the hurtful fission of your faults,

Grievous in time, concatenations of the ancient karmic law inherent from Adam,

Eruptive violations darkling with oblique refraction the bond of being—

Even the fierce incision of your sins dilate by virtue of your inner excellence,

Until the humanity possessed, the received delimitation from which all imperfection breeds, subsumes in your clear certitude of choice,

And in the tension trued what you became lifts to an ever greater salience of stature.

Caught on your term of truth the human good and the human bad fuse on the instant of an unequivocal assent,

And in that attestation you perfectly exist; in that essentiality you *are.*

Just as the general deficiency is healed only in the individual instance,
So have I seen humanity itself enlarged and amplified in your preemi-
nence,
Seen sin confirm you, unable to neutralize the latent and subsistent
truth that is your virtue,
But through a grace endowed become, clenched at your heart, the
very nexus of perfection,
Throwing into struck relief the magnitude, the matchless capacity of
unqualified assent,
Determining your arc and high trajectory to complicate, and hence
enrich, the modulated wonder of your worth.

And hence complete you—one and by one, as you stand free, the
function of your faults forces the surging shape of your perfec-
tion.
You tread them down like shards beneath your feet, or mount upon
them like tall steps to the divine,
Or laugh across them, seeing their useful uselessness in the august
majesty of Christ,
Who came in their delinquence, their work of emptiness, to forge
them in the long majestic function,
And hang them gleaming on the breast of God, deft talismen, the
singular medals of divine reprieve.

Brooked of that unrestrainable volition of response clearly they are
transformed upon the crest of your determination,
And are exalted, as saints' sins only serve to seal their sheer intrinsic
locus of perfection,
Annul themselves against the telling truth by which your virtue lives
transcendent,
Which makes you free, true to that searing shaping work within the
awesomeness that is your soul.

For your sins are generic, the inherited liabilities of time and your
place, the race's tortured trek through all eternity,
Bearing forward in its toil the repressed imbalance of attraction and
repulsion,

Crackling with compressed reaction, its multiple encounters with the
real,
Erupting the pent-up energies of individual volition, as the friable
element, the fractured human soul,
Gropes forward toward its synthesis, the ever-changing shape of
freedom and determination.

But your virtue is specific: in you alone I see those excellencies center
on the nodal zone of truth,
Personalized within the concrete dimension of gratuitous assent,
Individualized in the subsumed instant of precise volitional judgment,
Perfectly attuned to that comprehensive vision, that unfailing sup-
positum of taste,
And synthesized in the marvelous reflex of a sheer and unpremedi-
tated intuition.

For virtue in man is sourced not first in the demarcated, objectivized
act, the categorical preciseness of a factual achievement,
But rather in that naked rapacity in which the truth perceived is
grasped and registered,
The irrepressible élan of appetitive gusto, impelling the spirit on its
sheer incisive quest,
Attesting, by its instantaneous thrust, the flashed preponderance of
incipient being,
Which it so serves, so follows out, with an intense propensity, the
ravenous line of its just-glimpsed beatitude,
Constituent of the mystery of the Charity in which vitality and virtue
both are formed,
And out of which, wild with imminence, God does Himself achieve
the unmeasured marvel of His scopelessness.

And thus it is precisely in that high clear seizure of the instantaneous
Truth in which your sanctity is founded,
The fearlessness to seize in faith the brilliant instance of conceived
perception,
The disposition of that true interior alertness which never brooks the
imperfections hurting it,

But rather, acknowledging the God of All as Lord and Master, existential Truth,
Manifests perfections and imperfections each alike as they emerge,
the bright responses of a consummate assent.

Knowing that what is hidden will surely be seen, thrown clear in the
wide eye of day,
Knowing that the sins of the soul are no less there for never having
been committed,
You hold rather to that Lord's decisive provenance of incipient event
to prove the transformation, trusting Him wholly,
Than in the ego's hedging censures and prolaxed equivocal evasions.

For if "all the way to heaven is heaven," then all the way to sainthood
is sanctity,
Painfully teaching that the pure perfection, the luminous chasteness a
holy soul desires,
Was hardly the inchoate state we somehow feel began it, but is rather
The awesome imminence all thwarted nature desperately hopes for
end—
Achieved, if it is achieved, only upon the specific encounters of our
lives, instant by instant,
The ineluctable God bourning the precise gesture of intenseness, the
anguishing stroke
On which the total self, perfection on imperfection, is most acutely
gauged,
Until the soul, at last exposed, shudders under the terrible knowledge,
the inner-awesome truth,
As God defines it through those fierce contextual acts.

"Except your righteousness clearly exceeds the righteousness of
scribes and pharisees
Ye shall in no wise enter into the kingdom of heaven."
Obsessed, containing privately my abject attitudes, I seemed for a
time hardly to err,
And in my faultlessness shamed the shameless, a whited sepulcher, a
pious fraud.

297

But the saint is rather that jubilant one who in her absolute bound-
lessness of heart
Responds, contrite and joyous, and in the sheer response, proves
responsible.
Nor fears to stint the living sum of what she is, prescinding from that
scrupulous reactive guilt,
Whereas my cult of self entailed only a lofty image, momently
burnished,
Only a hollow shell, however crisply cut, however finely wrought.

For the saints are the lovers: seeing out of a love's excessiveness sin
shape its coiling strike,
Yet do they bear, they prosper, vice and its ruling virtue subsuming
the human province,
Our ancient legacy, Adam and Christ, the cockle and the wheat,
existent together.
This basic, incontrovertible reality, clinched in the fact, serenely
discloses, stark beneath the beauty, precisely what is there,
Man's every act, hinged on the fractured disposition, jagged beneath
the choice:
Saint Peter's folly, cruxed on the fierce determining complex, spawn
of the grinning archetype feeding denial.

Great because he bested, followed a flinchless faith to the jackal-maw
of fear,
But beaten because he boasted, took to himself the option of decision,
Spat out denial to save the polity of rescue, and saw the yawning sin
suck him down,
The o'er-mastering event, greater than he could know, clipped him,
and the cuckoo cock-crow raveled his riddling nerve—
Yet he stood forth, complexed of the guilt-in-faith, a man, and
crushed, and a saint,
Towering on the excessive pinnacle transparent, illumined in the
instancy of failure, his terrible triumphant heart.

So have I seen you weep and rejoice, in your tall moment of corruptive
truth, and stagger into Christ.

And see that deep in the heart's contrition not only are your sins made
    nothing (for this we hold in faith)
But burned through love gain an oblique reprieve bought back with a
    special grace,
Changed from the generic emptiness all sin can only be into the
    veritable agents of perfection,
Momently enforcing, through Christ's vast web of love, the actual
    effects of virtue,
And so redeemed, become the factuals of your greatest good, bright
    apertures of awareness,
Leaving you radiant, imponderably more potent than ever you were,
Incalculably more cogent than what you could have been or ever you
    groped them through,
Giving them back to God in the weaponry of grace, the *felix culpa* of a
    redemptive force etched across your heart in hieroglyphs of
    flame,
The *necessitum peccatum* Christ ever seeks out and needs, as the
    surgeon needs the wound,
To prove God's office of perfection, project His timelessness of truth.

It is in Him you touch completeness, and it is in you my incomplete-
    ness cries its lonely name,
As the imperishable image of Woman measures forever incomplete-
    ness in an unperfected man.
Over against my thwartedness of heart you stand, the epitome of
    realization,
The epiphany of that unconditional *fiat* God gave when He gave the
    world,
The Cosmic Rose of all reality, and which my slit-eyed self is stunned
    to glimpse,
But then expands, seizing out of its naked indigence the spacious
    valediction of your presence.

You stand inscripted as that ineluctable Other through which the
    unpent God marvels Himself.
No night but broods upon your dawn, no dawn but brooks against

your day,
No day but glitters on your sea, no sea but motions to your moon.
My life is crested to your tide-brunt like a keeling ship; I kedge your
deeps,
And through your island latitudes discern those mysteries the lunar
quest propounds.

But mostly it is as pole-star that your realism centers up my night of
faith.
Something unquenchable, something achieved to maximum intense-
ness and purity of repose, burns in your being,
Forcing my vague ambivalence to suck toward truth's center. Fas-
tened on your beam of truth
How can I waver or deflect and not deny the deepest instance that you
promise me I am?

And when you draw me on, although my fears shriek with an
anguished wail in terror at that path,
As the rust-bitten nail shrieks in its violence of extraction drawn from
the seasoned wood,
I summon the anguish up into one luminous point of pain, and press
on through,
Walking protected in the measure of your place in heaven, from
which your being, even now, anticipated,
Casts forth its fierce sheer light, its coiling, torch-like truth.

Thus when you rise at dawn from that deep couch of peace on which
your sleep is cast,
Your face reveals a wakefulness that day cannot confer, your glass
gives back a watchfulness no corporal beauty can define,
Your bath restores a youthfulness no natural ardor can have sourced,
For your uniqueness dwells upon no physicality alone, and your
benignant spirit
Enlivens a repose no unillumined flesh could actuate.

Your very bones bespeak perfection: the conformation of the living
face, the sutures of the skull.

Out of such depths the Aztec darkness casts its mystery beneath the
    clear Iberian ivory of your skin,
Endowing there the provocative Mexican movement, the modulent
    moment of mangoes and rum, the lambent flesh of the guave,
And those fierce poinsettias that stab the spirit with their perennial
    witness of the flesh.
Their passion daily proves you, and typifies the flashing surfaces
    beneath which glints
The irreducible essence, the marvelous mystery smouldering uncon-
    tainably on.

And whatsoever death the great indulgent God for you has framed,
    off there, in time's reprieve,
When HE WHO IS will take unto Himself His whole creation
    prefigured in your person,
Know that your image, at once conceived and explicated in the touch
    of time, never can truly die,
But lives immortal in that free transmuted world where all perfection
    is endowed, personified in you, His true creation,
That the stupefied world might thereby know, and knowing love, the
    instance of His vast concern.

And if I call you great, and if I call you holy, and if I say that even your
    sins enforce the sheer reality of what you are,
Know that I speak because in you I gaze on Him, by you I see Him
    breathe, and in your flesh I clasp Him to my breast.
So saying, let me confess the preeminent masterhood that is crea-
    tion's term,
And in your presence salute the transcendent Presence out of which
    you came.
Born of the Father, like Venus from the sea, you bear the beatific
    Ocean's witness of divine abyss,
To pierce, in time, through to the divine abyss from which you briefly
    dawned.

And at that time, though the world must lose the presence of your
    person, your fact will yet live on,

A thing achieved, hence irreducible, God's guerdon and signet that
    completeness, while His own, is yet endowed,
Because He made you in it, the prism of the greater Truth by which
    you are.
In such presence you persist, as in the lesser essence of this poem the
    movement of your breathfulness lives on,
But only as a gloss on what you are, existent only of my speech.

Pride of the presence, bride of the translucent Night, daughter of
    dawn and the resurgent Day,
Bestow on me once more your smile of essence, conferring in your
    grace my own reality,
Endowing as your perfect otherness my shape of man, that freed from
    my sickliness of soul,
I might, in Christ, achieve all that as man I must. And of such grace
Let me once more clasp in my arms the meaning of your fiery spirit,
    and burn upon my heart your perfect signature.

THE ROSE OF SOLITUDE

Her heart a bruise on the Christ-flesh suffered out of locked agonies of
    rebirth.
Her soul fierced inward upon the extravagant passion of woman cut
    between somber and radiant choices.
Her lips panting the Name of God as she thrusts out the tip of her
    tongue for one more drop of His nerving grace.

Solitary Rose! What wall could entomb her? She is all polish and
    ecstasy.
She is all passion, all fire and devotion. She is all woman, in love of
    God bitten by the rapture of God.
She sounds through my mind thirsting the inconceivable excellence of
    Christ.
I hear her feet like rain-clashes run the flat streets to do His will.

All ache. Her heart the glorified Wound. Her soul curls back on its
    pang as the toes of the Christ clutched back on that Nail.
In the stigmata of His gaze her love coils like the flesh on its iron, the
    love-ache of the opening.
When she utters the Holy Name you could never doubt God died for
    the love of man.

Solitary Rose! Unspeakable primacy! The masked and dangerous
    glint of implication!
The gleam of death in the knives of her desire! The crescendos thirsted
    in the strings of her passion!
I have seen in her eyes destinies expand and race out beyond the
    apogees of perfection!

She catches them all! Birds beak for her! In the click of her teeth she
    bites little pieces!
Dance! Dance! Never stint that torrential heart, girl and mother, holy
    immolation,
Free as none else of the vice of the self: that narrow hoard of un-
    broachable stinkings!

In the lift of her head earth glints and sparkles! The seethe of her voice
   is pure as the ecstasy of fire in ice!

Solitary Rose! The Spanish pride! The Aztec death! The Mexican
   passion! The American hope!
Woman of the Christ-hurt aching in moan! God-thirster! Beautiful
   inviolable well-deep of passion!
In the fiercest extravagant love is the tangible source of all wisdom!
In the sprint of your exquisite flesh is evinced the awesome reckless-
   ness of God's mercy!

PART THREE: DELIVER ME WHOLE

ON THE THORN

I

Gags. Thrids.
And in the thrid returning
The arrested stupration.

And I salute the long
Melody of affirmation.

As the Rose
Beheld in its raging invincibility
Concretes its essence.

Does time so devour that no ash returns?
Does the lightning of the sun
Striking irrefrangible cleavages,
Bestow the pure immutability of grace
On useless petals?

I have crouched out of sea-winds
Slumped behind boulders
To ponder her name.

II

And as woman
She walks in mystery,
And Mystery is God.

When she smiles
Creation seethes,
The ritual of rejuvenation,

The ecstasy of the Rose.

She is Woman.

Possessing reality
Wombed in her being,

The earth-shape
Refined in the fierce
Profundity of spirit:

Unfolding Rose.

III

Looking in on the laws of love
I know myself trapped in them.

Because I am a man of God
And given to God

Is it any sin
I cry out a woman's name?

IV

This is my fact:
I cry out a woman's name.

And have seen
God.
In that woman's face
Have known God's blaze.

Is it truly a sin
That her name is written,
Stroked in primal fire,
On my stultified heart?

V

What can I do?

I can love.

And in love
Keep faith.

What is faith
If I cheapen love
With servile fear?

What is fear,
That servility,

If, cheapening love,
It unnerves what I am?

VI

On this thorn, this anguish,
I turn nightlong.

As one set apart
I stand before men
Yet am I bound.

In the bind of my love,
Bound so to God,
Is the bond of her name.

In this wisdom,
Of this woman delivered,
I yet cling closed,
Captived on fear.

In this fear congealed
I deny what I am,
The truth that frees me.

Freed of truth,
Congealed in fear,
I grapple dust.
I bite straw.

VII

Do you call it disaster
That under the white
And the black of the friar
Burns a woman's name?

And where do you say it will end?

VIII

I am fifty years old,
The midpoint,
Of flesh but no lecher.

No lecher?
I turn on that thorn.

Fifty years old,
The cross-over.

Many a man has reefed on that surge.

But if latencies,
Emerging,
Create totalities of vision,
Is my love therefore proved?

This I believe:
God not only reads the heart
(To the core! To the core!)
But transforms the world through its energies.

IX

"When the devil
Can't find a way
He sends a woman."

So does God.

X

She arrives.
In one moment of warmth and infiltration
She envelops pickets.

What I thought were walls,
Defenses,
Dissolve in her presence,
Grey veils of mist.

I, celibate, stand in my flesh,
Am stormed by grace.

What the toil of my life,
Wrought between excess and abstinence,
Could never effect,
Is suddenly established.

XI

Then what do I hold?
I know this brink,
This threshold of passion
On which I founder,
Is nothing, not relevant.

My problem is primal.

If I am seized in passion
It is only because I fear the forbidden,
And crave what I fear.

She herself
Neither craves nor fears,
Is free.

She came into life
The fief of God.

So she remains.

XII

I have said before:
All the destinies of the divine
In her converge.

She stands at the center,
Or rather moves there,
Grasping in essence
The pulse of life.

She holds its key of secret
In her deep self-possession.

This truth is of faith.

XIII

Out of her, response
Flows like a gift.

In that gift she moves
Not above morality
But utterly within it.

Not destroying the law
But fulfilling it.

As if the Law itself
Were being achieved
At some awesome level.

If she makes mistakes
He corrects them.

It is that simple.

XIV

"Man judges the action.
God, the intention."
So quoth the prophet.

In the intention judged
What does God see?

Is my heart,
Poured of passion,
Impure?

What, in man, can purity be?

Not that I love
But *what* do I love?

In loving her
Do I love myself?

In such love,
Self-impelled,
Is love impaled?

I love: this I know.

Loving her,
Loving self in her,
What can deliver me?

To love her more
Is to love self less.
To love self less
Is to love God more.

To love selflessly
Is to love:

Him in her.

Amen.

                    xv

God speaks to her heart:

"What am I?
Pure act.

Only in act
Can you live in Me.

When I move you to live,
To *be*,

I do not expect
My sum of perfection.

Only I can be that.

But live out in grace
My fearlessness of truth
And be assured.

If you do so live,
Whatsoever the evil
Transmutes in My generosity.

The double effect
Subsumed in the pierce: grace,
The glimpsed beatitude.

I command.
I forgive.

It is that simple."

XVI

So does she do.

And I, celibate,
Stand hooked in her presence,
Unable to act.

She laughs and walks free,
Risking all.

I cower and cringe,
Risking nothing.

I crave and grab,
Risking nothing,
Losing all.

Passion propels me.
Grace informs her.

And she hews me out,

314

Forging out of my mode
One shape of man.

Cutting great gouts of rottenness
Out of my side,

Whole sloughs of sponginess
Chopped from my viscera.

These she delves with terrible strokes.
I scream in the purge.

XVII

And I love.

In my love
I cry out of my brutalized heart,
The contradiction riddling me,

Groping self-discovery out of my gash,
Struggling to clear my waters of soul.

Beyond the sexual force
My image of man—
Myself, friar and man,
In the eyes of the world:

In this am I riddled.

XVIII

Why, if I am true,

Am I unable,
Before the world,
To assert my truth?

I love a woman.

Riddled by love,
Encompassed by love,
Sustained by love—

Of a woman!

Here is a man
Who strove before the world
To perfect an image,
And was largely successful.

He is now impaled on it.

XIX

In His instance
God thirsts.

In God's thirst for love
Action redeems.

With that marvelous
Lift of her head
The Rose responds.

And the sheer response
Thrills reality,
Its flex of divestment.

I see.

Watching her move
My heart cramps on its catch,
Ineluctable.

She laughs.
She stands free.

Many a man has poured tears at her feet.

But when God chose the world
He chose her truth.

xx

O God & Riddler,
Why?

Is this sin?

I seek no sin.
I would never offend Thee.

I do offend Thee.

I would never offend Thee.

Do I offend Thee?

In her offend Thee?

Never!

I do offend Thee.

There is no offense in her,
How, then, do I offend Thee?

I do offend Thee.

XXI

Gags. Thrids.

Woman of God,
Once of this world,
What do you betoken?

Rose of Solitude,
Vessel of grace,
The mirror of perfection,
I salute your presence.

I salute your being,
And in your being
Acknowledge your flesh.

I salute your flesh
And in your flesh
Acknowledge your spirit.

I salute your spirit
And in your spirit
Behold God's grace.

XXII

Woman, whom I love,
But cannot marry.

Whom I touch,
But may not bed.

Whom I praise
But never possess.

In your act,
Your stroke of deliverance,

When at last you deliver me,
Deliver me entire.

Deliver me whole!

THE UNDERLYING TORSION

A lull of no wind.
And out of the ashen
Death-drugged sky
A drizzle for thaw,
A feathery drift: the vague
Fingers of life-reviving quest
Tracing the snow.

Over the beech forests,
Over the hickory woods and the sap maple thickets
That did freeze in the awful zero of cold:
The slow lease of nascent relaxation,
A soft uncramping.

And I think of the svelte
Hills of California, their lambent nudeness,
Prone on the shore beside the dalliance of beaches,
Redisposing in their immemorial womanly way
The underlying torsion of the earth's old flaw,
The lock-jawed lips of the San Andreas fault.

And here, far away, in the frozen
Core of New England,
Ice in the veins of the Puritan heart,
I hear the snow
Slip from the branches,
And bring back to my mind
The subtropical presence,
The death-dissolving movement in wisdom and in warmth,
Of one out there
Who laughs her way through the spring-haunted glades,
Bestowing on all whom she touches,
Given out of her maiden-heart and her mother-eyes,
God's gaze, God's liberating look.

Dover, Massachusetts

320

THE VISION OF FELICITY

And the terrible
Pang of the heart unhinged,
Bereft of its sources.

Out of the smashed
Light; out of the hard
Unmalleable, abstract
Ferocity of the streets;

Out of the depraved
Human face, horribly
Emptied of its beatitude—

I behold. I behold.

I behold the vision of felicity
And the insuperable human grace.

As one who after mindless torment
Sees surcease in the smile of gratitude,
The plenitude of peace.

Give me my love!
This cry, this cruciform.

Give me back the beauty!

Give me my ache of love
Out of this emptiness!

From the belled
Hell, from the brass
Inferno:

Give me the center back
Of my soul!

New York City

321

I EAT LIFE BACK

And her eyes
Break back death. At the grave's
Ravenous repossession
She sways and ripples,
Unstemmable.

    I have heard the tomb of earth
    Breathe its stain of fetor.

But she stamps,
She clips her foot and bats fly.
She snaps two fingers;
The grave cracks on its oath.
In the No! of her head
Its brittle harmonics
Chip and vanish.

    I have heard the sow of death
    Sigh, its jaw
    Peeled in terror, slaking
    Unspeakable earth motives
    As it gags and thrids.
    I have shocked to dread.

But her eyes
Blaze of that truth rebuking deceit,
And I eat life back.

PART FOUR: WHAT FREEDOM IS

FROM THE ROCK UNTOMBED

I

From the rock untombed,
The dawned resurrection.

Icon of the womb,
Matrix of the mother.

Between the gates of stone,
The bone portal,

Terrible in truth
The Word rejoices!

II

The blunt hand groped
The cleft of Being.

Through the porch of bone
Reeled the drunken soldier.

Rude in the solemn weal
Stumbled the sodden roisterer.

Senseless his shunt,
The throat of silence.

Mindless his maze,
The womb of stillness.

Blinded, the upstart stumbles.

Terrible in truth
The Word rejoices!

III

Let the hand be wrung
That fouled the placid water.

Root out this wrong,
Rout this wrath.

Chopped, the stolid finger.

Axe of stone,
The bladed granite.

Righteous his retribution,
Is not? Is not?

Terrible in truth
The Word rejoices!

IV

Let peace prevail,
Its pureness of presence.

On the cliff above the sea,
The solitary star,

Scarved in cloud,

Sinks and closes,

Blunt hand is stanched,
Its wrong to ponder.

Heartskin is slit,
Membrane of the senses.

Out of that cave
The blunderer is born.

Terrible in truth
The Word rejoices!

v

In the womb of the Mother
The Word conceives.

In the Chalice of God
Is born the Self-Conceiver.

There burns the light,
There dawns the luster,

Where mind was drunken,
A sensual dream,

Aura of illusion
Is mist-veil vanished.

Terrible in truth
The Word rejoices!

VI

O lion of the heart,
Rager and pursuer,

Where the lioness roams,
Nights of striped lightning.

O longing of the lions,
The bronze lion lust,

Stretched and toiling,
A sensual spasm,

The tawny coupling,
The clinging, the clawing,

Tumescent in torment,
The drench of stolt desire.

In the song of sex
The lionness lapses,

The lions lash,
But the turbulence passes.

Terrible in truth
The Word rejoices!

VII

In the sealed Rock,
The tomb of resurrection

In the mother-womb,
The living chalice,

The Word awaits,
Unborn, unresurrected,

Beyond the pang of birth,
Beyond the pain of death,

The single substance:

Before the mother-womb,
Before the father-phallus,

Before the thunder sounded
The birth of malice:

Terrible in truth
The Word rejoices!

VIII

Out of the Rose restored,
The round returning.

Bless the murder-hand,
The brutal member,

Blunderer, betrayer,
The stunned assaulter,

The drunken soldier,
Stumbler on peace.

O Throne of God!

O Seat of Wisdom!

Nascent of night,
The perfect plenty.

Hushed, the chambered glory.

Terrible in truth
The Word rejoices!

THE RAGING OF THE ROSE

And the Rose
Rages. Over the Cross
The thorns of denial
Rebuke the egoism of prepossession.
In the imminence of assent
The bloom of essence, actualized,
Unsheaths the storms of existence. Thus it is
That anguish, self-cancellation
Yields into being
The multifoliate particularities of the whole.

In the presence of person
The Rose, invincible, rages and affirms.
Being and Becoming
Realize the sublime synthesis,
The ecstasy of presence.

Son and Mother,
The self-sacrificing God
Immolated on the Tree.
Christ and the Cross
Incarnating irreducibly
The ecstasy of the Rose.

Bride of the world, a nuptial
Consummated unendingly
On the Sword of Spirit.

Tremulous flesh,
Alive with instinct and potentiality,
Deflowered instant by instant:
Over and over the unslakable scepter
Thirsting through the nightfall of the flesh
Its subsistent good.

Flesh and spirit,
Spirit and flesh,
Transmuted together,
Sealed in Christ,
The indwelling.

                    He gazes
Out of the very pores of the skin,
The irreducible
Subjectivity of person
Transcending, exceeding in depth,
The whole world of objects,
The whole world of subjects.

                    *

Dance! Dance!
Dance on the Cross of God,
The cruciform of the Rose!
Dance out the fierce exultancies.
Dance out the rivering apogee of time and its deceptions.
Dance in the heart's redemptive craze
That seizes the shackles of fallen worlds
And annuls their prison.

In the elemental pound of explicit hope
The world restores.
Under the feet of a thousand triumphs
The Cross renews.

In the life of the Rose, the pulsant
Point of mystical intuition,
God immolates Himself,
Makes Himself new. Form
Constellates Being, as the cone of Creation,
Specified,
Meets the cone of the Uncreated,

Specified.

She exults.

*

And she keeps, she abides, the long
Ecstasy of affirmation, the dynasty of the Rose,
Its raging invincibility, its articulate
Force, its clear
Ethos of truth. As the sun
Bursting out under cloud, its plunge toward earth,
Burns, the coal of itself
One ruby for sunset,
And the conflagration, the rose refulgence,
Purifies the West.

Spurn, in my mind's
Solitary eye,
Voiceless,
Constellated,
The insuperable body
And the sequent grace,
The poem
Breaks,
And out of these long-locked lips,
Out of this throat,
These ventricles,
Toll the throes of celebration,
The canticle of the Rose!

*

And I
Am free:
Because the spirit
In me

Cries out to the Christ
In her, and is appeased—
The long
Shout of jubilation,
The sole
Syllable of delight.

In the mutuality of this gaze
His cry of love,
Of anguish,
Out of the travail of sensuality
Glimpsing itself beyond the Beloved,
Crying out through the inarticulate web of the senses
Of what is not sensate, rejoicing
Under its cringe of anguish,
Its moan of bliss.
The unbelievable prolongation of the trill of contingency,
An unimpeachable love: this our gasp of delight,
Christ's oath of truth: God's cry.

*

And so He listens, He answers Himself.
Across long riverings of time He has come.
He arrives,
He gazes,
The smile of these essences bridging Being,
His own meaning is.

We are the metaphors of His certitude,
His power to perfect.
We are the symbols of His supremacy.
We are the mutually inflected beatitude
That yields Him contingency,
Prompts His strike.
In our single gaze
His glimpse beyond finitude

Opens existence.
Not ego, the finite principle,
But presence, Self, *atman:*
The mode of the infinite.

Two egos,
Selfed in unison, moded on the subsistence of Christ,
His single Isness.
She taught me: how one is free,
Possessing freedom in subsistence,
What freedom is.
I taught her: how the crest of emotion,
That freedom,
Is crowned on the undersurge of intellectual passion,
Which is depth.

She taught me: what deliverance is,
The freedom that is salvation.
In truth, in truth,
That the free
Is freedom as truth
Is being,
The crest of release
That liberates freedom
In the primacy of response,
The *act* of existence.

As act, being: His *esse:* to be.

So she: I.
In us: He is.
We Three:
Free.

*

For in her

All the defects of Woman find their apogee of relevance
And are transfigured: jealousy, suddenness, curiosity,
Vainness, pique, tears, dissimulation, folly—
Ingredients of the essential mystery
Femininity is. Her utterness
Canonizes them each through her sheer
Assertion of being,
Constituents of the feminine mode
That seek their power of reflection,
Ornaments of spontaneity
The scandal of masculine gravity
Established on the due subordination of woman
And the rejection of spontaneity of love.
These she defies,
Not by insolence, as the adventuress
Controverts the stunned world of man
And appropriates its fixtures,
But in the primacy of response,
Essential to the whole of feminine nature
And indigenous to its truth.
Presenting each
To the face of God
She dances,
As the irrepressible daughter
Dances in the doting father's eye,
Supremely confident,
Roguishly certain of what delights him,
Because she knows she typifies
What fatherhood never can be,
And so adores.

*

You emerge,
Unwombed of the world.
Elemental as the elemental earth,
As lava under the shelves,

As the river in the gorge.
Fierce as the sun, fierce as the high-falling light.
Sudden as waterfalls poured over ledges.
Uncontainable as the swirling torrents of air that plow the globe.
Awesome as the immeasurable storms bourning in from far shores.
Ineluctable as the sea, as restless and as eternal.
Beautiful as being because you possess being.
Elusive as the bird escaped from the fowler.
Wise as the Church because you possess the Church,
For in you, She is.
In you
She achieves Her presence,
Presages Her future.

For out of your womb
Children have come
As souls come forth from the font of baptism.
Out of your heart
Love has come
As Christ came forth from the womb of His mother.
Out of your mind
Wisdom has come
As Idea comes forth from the mind of God.
Out of your lips
Truth has come
As Bread comes forth from the hands of Christ.

Rose! O rareness of the revealed!

Dance! Dance out the truth of being, as act and existence!
Dance up the lineal measurement of time to its quintessence!
Beat it up into synthesis!
Under the storm of your heels
Pound to perfection!
Make it be!
Establish it in your movement,
The perdurable moment that cannot die!

Incarnate it!
Divinize it in your fierce unquenchable essence!
Confer beatitude upon it!
Immortalize it in your glance,
Your look and your laughter!
By the kiss of your lips,
By the ecstasy of your breath,
Re-create it anew!

O clear expression of beauty!
O melody of existence!

Rose!
Reality unfolded!

On the four wings of the Cross,
In the ecstasy of crucifixion,
In the blood of being,
In the single burn of beauty

BE!

So that
In you,
The consummate
Vision of Other:

In you
I AM!

PART FIVE: I ORIGINATE DEATH

THE FACE I KNOW

"The face I know
Becomes the night-black rose."

And I cry out of a shambling of pain,
A clotting of anguish.

                  Great tongs
Tear rents of speechlessness
Cut from my lips.

I drunkenly stagger. I flay
Segments of numbness.
A shuff of wretchedness
Tatters my shanks.

      *

And once more in my life
I keen the sheerest grief, the one
Chagrin, an ecstasy of loss:
The pure privation.

I sing the song of a man
Put down, gulled
Between woman and the will
Of the world.

       Demolished
By all that opened him out.

       Abandoned
By that which edified Hell.

Flaked shreds
Cull splints of ridiculousness
Crackling like nut-brickle
Under my soles.

Sunk fragments of pain
Chip flintage of itch
Through my fact of death.

     *

And I do. I originate
Death. I eat
The must of it foul.

Champing its substance of acridness
Crunched in my teeth
I gulp savor.

"These ones have thorns,"
Said the vendor, taking coin. "Careful
They don't up and stick you
For your pains. They cut quick."

I hugged in my arms the wild roses,
Their crushed abundance
A stifling mockery
Warning the air,
A liquid lament.

Then I felt nails pierce my palms
And I knew it was over.
I knew she was gone.

     *

And what kills in me

I kill in my life.

What slivers me through
I seize up and devour.

I am freed. I rush
The rampage, the turmoil
Of deliverance.

                  Out of this
Smashed hurt
I grab windfalls of freedom.

I go forward in death.
The creative death we call Life
Is God. Is death in God.

       *

Eat me Christ. I lip blood
For my worship. Grind me like shuck
Between the teeth of beasts
Carnivorous God, great cannibal
Of life, dark glutton of death.
Chaunk man's flesh for victuals:
I am your food.

O Jesus of the bitten brow,
The rat-nibbled feet,
Tombed amid vermin and lewd
Varmints of earth!

Gopher-gnawn God of worms and men,
Conceiver and destroyer,
Great famisher of life:
I lip your mouth!

And I crawl out of here.
I inch out of this place.
I wrig long tunnels of darkness.
I spot daylight, promising
The purity of pain.

Give me my pain for purge.
Give me my hurt to heal me on,
Lord and Master,
Burn me black and burn me brittle
But slip me deliverance.

O self! self!
Crippler and ensnarer,
The heart's bestial oath!
O self-deceiver!
O man of fictions!
Whence freedom?
What anguish
Is its aim?

*

And I crawl.
I will get there.
Like a clubbed snake
I hitch toward freedom.
Out of this skin, this slough,
Across these illusions,
Upon this blood.

No law
But the law of deprivation.

No hope

But the hope of deliverance.

No curse
But the curse of the uncaptived.

                *

And my life
Comes round. The great millstone
Of exaction, flint-hearted Capricorn
Plunging toward Pisces
And the torpid fish.

Twenty years gone
I knocked my breast
Over Waldport water,
Rolling those hideous
Moon-ringed eyes,
On the cliffed
Sea-shelf
Searching for source.

Dip down! Dip
Down! Dip . . .

                A groping
Between crude flanges of hurt
Crackling on deprivation:
The willfulness of woman,
My own conceit.

Crippled. My crippling
Teaching me. Hunching through
To the true nothingness,
That utterness,
The not-to-be-known
Abstract reality

That lies beyond nature.

And every fleck of prime Being
Whirls up;
A measureless movement
Refashions the world.

*

Dance. Dance.
Dance out the troubled dream,
The intervals of silence.

Dance up the wastage of time,
The shuff of existence.

Rose of the real.
Rose of the reddest heart,
The bloodiest beauty.

Rose of response,
The total reach,
The rarest renouncement.

Somewhere you slip through sweeps of ecstasy,
Your savagery of truth
Skewered on the flint knife
That crucifies your heart.

The Spanish pride. The Aztec
Death. The Mexican passion.

Somewhere the light falls forward out of your face
Stabbing your lips.

Unpossessible Rose!
The black beat of God,

Pure strippings of fate.
I have spun in and out of your dream and been annulled.
I start through raptures of passion.
Detonations of hurt
Pummel my heart.

Wherever I go
The burn of that beauty
Brands me, bludgeons me.
I am thrown.
I slew sideways.
Grinning I go down.

Getting up I mouth
Blasphemes of incomprehension,
The stutter of gall.

A forked, naked man?

One spasm of pain in the world's womb.
One wince in the dark.

THE AFTERGLOW OF THE ROSE

As what goes out
Toward rare prospects,
Remote propensities.

Hush, heart.

Something is done.
Something sears on to new tilts,
New densities.

Hunch: hurt.

Something goes on.
Far themes of surcease
Transform the stabs of protestation,
Valorize the pang.

All the tentacles of attachment,
Root-hairs of resistance,
Transmute toward peace.

O heart! heart!

Let the body's truth
Strike defts of realness
Through the soul's shocked depth.

Let symbols,
Transformations,
Coil spheres of wholeness
In the heart's crude thrash.

What persists?

Voices.

Celebrations.

Then hunch!
Be shut of it!

For she leaves in her wake
A long path of pureness,
The afterglow of the Rose.

As the footprint of Christ
On the calmed water
Remains immortal,

So her presence,
Gone,

On my soul's
Cowed sea,

Prolongs its truth.

EPILOGUE

Cold gropes the dawn. Time wavers on the interdicted face.
   A sovereignty of distance shapes and fashions
   The contours of those long abandoned passions.
Charred fragments of desire flake upward from that place.

Outside, the visionary rainfalls veil the day.
   The mystic semblance of an ancient sorrow
   Trembles the nighttime of our vast tomorrow.
Reluctant as the light they fade and glide away.

Her face re-enters time. God of all tangled deeps
   Revokes the sureties of old reliance,
   Darker than the stonefalls of defiance.
She murmurs in her dream, and stirs herself, and sleeps.

EPILOGUE:
WHO IS SHE THAT LOOKETH FORTH AS THE MORNING

Who is she that looketh forth as the morning,
Fair as the moon, clear as the sun,
Terrible as an army with banners?

—THE SONG OF SONGS

Rising among the stampings of the sea
She shakes the lifting light about her throat;
Her arms keep coolness with the stinging breeze,
And waves cup to her like a heeling boat.

Floating a risk of tresses on her nape
She wades the drift, and shaken of it, sways,
Treads riftages of brine, and treading swings;
She clicks her fingers on the birth of days.

Her shoulders sleek of sunlight and her breasts
Sculpt sea-troughs from the shoals of running seas;
Her narrow ankles split the stunning surf,
Barracuda slashes landward through her knees.

Lips glitter prophecies in waterlight,
Chromatic glints, bright oceanic flame,
Presaging triumphs and the doom of kings;
They sigh submission when she breathes their name.

Visage to visage, brow to burning brow,
They will fall forward through volcanic fire,
Rapt in the shudder of her vast embrace,
The drench of her insatiate desire.

She is the Mother of Life, Mistress of Death,
Before her feet the tiger coughs and dies,
And the bony elephant gives up the boast
Of those vast passions that once filmed his eyes.

Savage and awesome as the birth of suns
She treads a tumult on the stippling shore,
Churning the fleets of caliphs through her thighs,
And drowning the sailors that her daughters bore.

She is the Mother of Life, of Death the pride,
Nothing in nature broke that Maidenhead:
Man's glory entered life between her knees,
Yet does she keep inviolable the Bed.

Svelte goddesses usurped her place, but fell
Sweating with lovers in a flint embrace.
She holds herself immaculate apart;
The Spirit's expectation burns her face.

Yet lovers all must wanton of her will;
Out of her passion children shoulder birth.
The savage grips her in his groaning wife;
She takes her tribute of the teeming earth.

Dung and all darks are hers to ordinate,
The thirst of mules, the semen of the stag,
Beat of the flesh and the flesh's diffidence,
The sperm-swift cuspèd in the dreaming bride.

When lances break the ridges of the bone
Hers is the hand, and when the widow weeps,
Hers the invincible will that took the man,
Shovelling the tall dead for her windrow heaps.

She is the Mother of Life, the Queen of Death,
Her only Lover lives beyond the skies,
Coming to cover under the lightning flash,
The impregnation of the prophet's cry.

Upon a night of geysers by a sea
When the dead lay listening in their soundless pall,
And angels, fallen, shrilled the monody,
Strophe on strophe of their ancient gall,

She was accosted on a lonely hill
By what no man conjectured: in her womb
She bore the impact and the sacred Seed:
Pure passion broke the sceptre of the Tomb.

Fire and thunder, fury at the source,
The blood's distemper and the mystic cry:
She took the wild Lover face to face;
She drank the danger of the brutal sky.

Prey of the lightning flash she dropped, consumed,
A votive-victim and a sacred feast;
Spun to the black and leopard-throated wind,
The Spirit cupped her like a roaring beast.

That was the night the Son of God was struck
Deep in man's flesh, and left the body stunned,
Thrown by the Holy Spirit's aching lust,
Godhead and woman incommensurately oned.

What she gave birth to was halved of herself
And halved of Spirit, and would offer proof,
Searching God's cross out through the stark event
That immolates her instinct in His truth.

And when He mounts the cross-hilt of her flesh,
And nerve to membrane, joint to muscle bleeds,
She spits the seeds of passion through her teeth,
And sucks the wound that in His body seethes.

All night the little foxes cry her name,
In dunes beyond the sentinels of the streets;
But the gaunt Cross, divested of its love,
Milks blood like stinging rain between her teats.

Hewn of the digger's art, the stony slot
Seals flesh her womb kept like a doubled fist,
The man wrapped in His bridal cloth prescinds
The indentured breed from Time's slab-guttered list.

Now in the night the lovers seize her shape,
Each in the other's arms compassion taking.
Storming God's gate they hurl their lives aloft,
And harrow hell with that tremendous slaking.

Bride and the bridegroom, stroke on stroke surpassing,
The sexual agon or the heart's contrition,
Evoke the awe, induce, draw down the dream,
Compel the Spirit's awesome dereliction.

She is the Mother: in her womb the God
Burgeons Himself anew and tramples death;
And lifts her, plunging in the blaze of birth,
And shutters with His lips her surging breath.

AFTERWORD

"EVERSON / ANTONINUS:
CONTENDING WITH THE SHADOW"

ALBERT GELPI

In a review almost a decade ago, I hailed *The Rose of Solitude* as the most significant volume of religious poetry since Robert Lowell's *Lord Weary's Castle* twenty years before, and argued that Brother Antoninus' poetry was more profoundly Christian than Lowell's because it was more Incarnational, whereas Lowell's lapse from Catholicism stemmed from his difficulty in accepting the awesome, violent paradoxes of the central Christian mystery. Lowell ended up caught in the ambiguities of agnosticism, revising and adding to his random *Notebook* in the same, confined fourteen-line conventions. And now, with Antoninus' early, pre-Catholic poetry, written as William Everson, available still in the collection *The Residual Years*, and with this new and complete collection of poems spanning his Dominican years, I would venture the judgment that if T. S. Eliot is the most important religious poet in English in the first half of the twentieth century, Everson / Antoninus is the most important religious poet of the second half of the century.

The extreme contrasts between those two poets point to a symptomatic tension in the religious commitment. The differences are less doctrinal than temperamental: Eliot the conservative classicist submitting the weaknesses of the individual to the reasonable authority of tradition and institutional structures in order to absolve him from the exigencies of personality; and Everson, the romantic individualist, trusting reason less than the undertow of passion and instinct to write out a life-long poem, as Whitman did a century ago, of the struggles with himself to realize himself.

Many would argue that authentic religious experience must be distinguished from intellectual commitment to an ecclesiastical structure, and that the great religious poetry of the first half of the century came not from Eliot but from such figures as Ezra Pound, D. H. Lawrence, Robinson Jeffers. Such a statement is not fair to Eliot, since the philosophical meditations of *Four Quartets* do derive from genuine religious experiences. However, the distinctions between modes of religious sensibility postulated bluntly above is fundamental and revealing.

For what links the other three poets and Everson together, for all their admitted differences, is precisely what Eliot shrank back from as from the devil: a sourcing of self in the Dionysian unconscious rather than Apollonion consciousness; a faith in the forces—pre-rational, irrational, suprarational, what you will—instinct in nature and emergent in the human psyche. Their poetry functions in good part to articulate the eruption into consciousness of the unconscious energies which are for them the source and secret of life. Pound recovered such primal experiences in the Greek myths and the mysteries of the occult; Lawrence, like Whitman, in the divine carnality of the sexual drive; Jeffers, in the pantheism which sees in the sea and rocks and creatures of the shore "the brute beauty of God" beyond the predatory violences of the egoistic mind and will. And in the poetry of each such psychological and spiritual explorations led to open form and free verse, as the poem discovered its definition.

By contrast, the explicitly Christian poets of the twentieth century have, by and large, tended to stress the constraining limits of a radically flawed creation through which the refractions of the Spirit penetrate at best tenuously and elusively, and they have generally insisted on working within the limitations of formal conventions as a way of testing and fixing "hints and guesses," as Eliot described our experience of the Incarnation. The means and the meaning, the norms and the measure have therefore been ruminative, guarded, Apollonian in the main. The elaborated patterning of the *Quartets* conveys not just the timeless moments which have transformed Eliot's life, but also the abiding disillusionment with temporal existence which qualifies and survives the moments of transcendence. Marianne Moore's intricately artful syllabics are a discipline to verify and regulate the allegorist's reading of natural experience in moral and religious terms. The virtuosity of Richard Wilbur's carefully maintained poise and symmetry epitomizes his conviction that the Incarnation calls us to attend to "things of this world" for "their difficult balance" of body and spirit. The religious pieces which conclude Allen Tate's long spiritual travail are written in Dante's *terza rima* in aspiration towards a faith that seems all but beyond his grasp. In Robert Lowell's Catholic poems, alternately stretched and clenched on their metrical and metaphorical designs till they threaten to wrench themselves apart, the Spirit moves to save human nature in death, which saves it from natural corruption; for him, the advent of the Incarnation spells Apocalypse. John Berryman enacted his religious anxiety through the knotted syntax and studied cadences of Anne Bradstreet and of Henry, and even after his late return to the Church his poems vacillate between prayers for patience and impatient anticipation of breaking free of the human tragedy.

It is the very history of religious—especially Christian—poetry in the twentieth century, with its fixation on human fallibility and its consequent insistence on necessarily prescribed forms, that makes Everson's poetry seem radical, original, transformative. Most of the Dionysians in recent poetry—Allen Ginsberg, Jack Kerouac, Lawrence Ferlinghetti, like Hart Crane in the twenties—have used alcohol or drugs for release into vision, but Ralph Waldo Emerson, who opened the way for Whitman and all the later Dionysian poet-prophets, was the first to condemn such "*quasi*-mechanical substitutes for the true nectar," which would end in "dissipation and deterioration." The distinctiveness of Everson's achievement springs, rather, from the Dionysian character of his Christianity. This has evolved in two complementary phases: from the beginning, his surrendering to primal experience until at last it yielded him the Christian mystery; and his surrendering, then, to the Christian mystery so unreservedly that it enflamed and illuminated, below and above structured rational consciousness, that dark area, at once the center and circumference of psyche, where passion and spirit reveal themselves as personhood incarnate.

*

How did this transpire through more than sixty years of living and forty of poetry? William Everson's life has been punctuated again and again by interruptions, abrupt changes and seeming reversals. What has been the continuity? Born in 1912 in Sacramento, growing up in California's San Joaquin Valley, his grandfather the founder of an evangelical sect in Norway, his stern father an agnostic, his mother a Christian Scientist, Everson was a dreamy, withdrawn young man, but in 1934 he discovered the master whose work made him a poet: Robinson Jeffers. Jeffers represented an "intellectual awakening and the first religious conversion, all in one." "When Jeffers showed me God in the cosmos, it took and I became a pantheist," and "that pantheism was based on a kind of religious sexuality," a sense of the universal life-force compelling all things in the sexual rhythm. Reading Lawrence a few years later confirmed for him the sacredness, even divinity, of natural life, but stylistically his lines adapted the expansive free-verse of Jeffers to his own verbal movement and timbre. Everson married Edwa Poulson in 1938 and began cultivating his own vineyard in the Valley. "August" is characteristic of much of the early poetry in its identification with the female earth so deep that masculine intellect relinquishes sovereignty and the poet yields virginal to the God of Nature:

> Smoke-color; haze thinly over the hills, low hanging;
> But the sky steel, the sky shiny as steel, and the sun shouting.
> The vineyard: in August the green-deep and heat-loving vines
> Without motion grow heavy with grapes.
> And he in the shining, on the turned earth, loose-lying,
> The muscles clean and the limbs golden, turns to the sun the lips and the
>   eyes;
> As the virgin yields, impersonally passionate,
> From the bone core and the aching flesh, the offering.

He has found the power and come to the glory.
He has turned clean-hearted to the last God, the symbolic sun.
With earth on his hands, bearing shoulder and arm the light's touch, he
 has come.
And having seen, the mind loosens, the nerve lengthens,
All the haunting abstractions slip free and are gone;
And the peace is enormous.

That peaceful harmony was shattered by the Second World War. Everson's pantheism made him a pacifist; death and destruction in nature were part of the ecological cycle, but in the human order were violational because egoistic and malevolent. The figure of the bloody warrior from his Nordic ancestry stalks the poetry of the late 30's as the Shadow-inversion of the feminine pacifist-pantheist. But when the holocaust broke, Everson retreated to nature and spent the years 1943-1946 as a forester in an Oregon camp for conscientious objectors. "The Raid" describes war as rape, and "The Hare" acknowledges the Shadow in himself with the awareness, "fathered of guilt," that we are all killers. Still, fascinated as he was and remained with assertive masculinity (Jeffers was similarly ambivalent), he chose the C.O. camp in the name of his feminine suscep-tibilities.

But only at great cost. "Chronicle of Division" recounts the personal crisis in the global disorder: the breakup of his marriage and the dissolu-tion of his previous life. In 1946 he came to San Francisco to join the pacifist-anarchist group around Kenneth Rexroth who as writers were opposing the established academic poets and critics in the cause of open form and spontaneity. There he met and married the poet-artist Mary Fabilli. The sequences *The Blowing of the Seed* and *The Springing of the Blade* hymn their union and move the nature mysticism of the earlier poetry more explicitly into the area of human sexuality. But she was a lapsed Catholic undergoing a rebirth of faith, and through her ordeal Everson found his own life unexpectedly altered and clarified:

> It was my time with Mary Fabilli that broke both my
> Jeffersian pantheism and my Lawrencian erotic mysti-
> cism. She personalized this, her whole touch was to
> personalize, to humanize. . . . Also the intuition to
> which her course led me is that my mystical needs, my
> religious needs, which had not really been met in my
> pantheism, could only find their solution in the more
> permeable human context, and in a ritual and a rite, and
> in a mythos that was established in a historical con-
> tinuity.

At Midnight Mass, Christmas 1948, Everson was overwhelmed, psychologically, almost physically, by the divine presence in the tabernacle, and that mystical encounter led directly to his conversion the next year. However, by a grotesque twist of irony, the previous marriages of both partners and the prevailing Church procedures at the time made it impossible for them to remain husband and wife. *The Falling of the Grain* deals with the wrenching ironies and the overriding commitment which underlay their decision to separate. Two years later he entered the Dominicans as a lay brother and served for almost nineteen years, during which time the poems written as Brother Antoninus made him a figure in the San Francisco Renaissance and the Beat Generation and a charismatic presence at readings on campuses around the country.

In fact, Everson's conversion and Antoninus' monasticism did not so much "break" his pantheism and erotic mysticism, as break them into a new set of circumstances and a new psychological and spiritual dimension. Now his life was centered on the Incarnation. Not an isolated historical event, but a daily miracle: the ongoing infusion of Creator into creation, supremely expressed in Jesus, the God-Man. The individual hangs on that cross, where all the contradictions of the human condition take on new consequence. The natural and the supernatural, soul and body, sexuality and spirituality—the Incarnation means that those seeming polarities, often vehemently at cross purposes, are meshed at the point of tension.

From the human point of view the Incarnation cancelled out Original Sin, so that God could redeem man from the sinfulness which was part of his freedom. Everson had seen the killer in himself; like Eliot, he knew that the fallible will needed to be curbed by ethical restraints and external norms lest creative freedom become oppression or anarchy; and his penitential bent sought the stricter discipline of monasticism. But from God's perspective the Incarnation is the completion of the creative act. On the one hand, God could be seen as driven to descend into flesh to save soul from body: the vision of Lowell and Eliot. But on the other hand God could be seen as having saved man in his human condition: not Spirit charging into flesh but Spirit embodied; not sinful flesh but transfigured body. The implications of this mystery were tremendous and dangerous, and Everson was driven to search them out. For when God became man, did He not submerge himself in the sexual element? In fact, was not sexuality the manifestation of that submersion? Had He not chosen from eternity to move in and through the sexual polarity, so that our sexual natures disclose their divine impulsion? Then in the heart-beat, pulse-throb, sex-urge, the Incarnation unfolds the contingencies of time and space, and subsumes them. Now Antoninius found himself confronting these paradoxes in exactly the situation which would test them most severely: separated from the wife who was the saint of his conversion, bound by his own election to a vow of celibacy.

Consequently the poetry of Brother Antoninus is almost obsessively concerned with the Feminine—that is, not only women, but his own sexuality and the feminine component in his psyche which mediates his passional, instinctual and poetic life. Decades before he had read Jung's psychology his poetry was recording his own often conflicting encounter with the major archetypes: in the psyche of a man, the Shadow, who represents his dark, repressed, even violent aspects; the Anima, the woman within, who is his soul and leads him into engagement with his erotic and spiritual potentialities; and, most dimly, the Self, that achieved and transcendent personhood realized through the resolution of polarities, who reveals himself as the God within and of whom, Jung says, Jesus is the symbol and reality. Everson's poetry through the war had enacted an initial rejection of the Shadow; now the Anima became the primary archetypal focus in the struggle toward transcendence.

In the Fictive Wish, written in 1946 before meeting Mary Fabilli, is a marvelous evocation of what Everson was already recognizing as "the woman within":

> Wader,
> Watcher by wave,
> Woman of water;
> Of speech unknown,
> Of nothing spoken.
>
> But waits.
>
> And he has,
> And has him,
> And are completed.
>
> So she.

But what was the monk to make of her? Often she came to him as the dark temptress, allied with his own lustful Shadow and luring him on to what must now be sexual sin. Many of the poems in *The Crooked Lines of God*, written soon after converting and becoming a Dominican, excoriate the flesh, and the poems in the first half of *The Hazards of Holiness* churn in the frustration not just of lust but of his passionate nature. They recount, Everson has said, his own "dark night." "A Savagery of Love" makes Mary Magdalene, the patroness of the Dominicans, the image of the purified Anima, redeemed from whoredom into "a consumate chasteness," her passion focussed on the Passion of the Incarnated God.

Now, in that divine identification the Anima could express her passionate nature. In "The Encounter" and several other remarkable poems towards the end of *Crooked Lines* Antoninus becomes the woman before God, his / her whole being called into activity by His totally mastering love. "Annul in Me My Manhood" opens with the prayer:

> Annul in me my manhood, Lord, and make
> Me woman-sexed and weak,
> If by that total transformation
> I might know Thee more.
> What is the worth of my own sex
> That the bold possessive instinct
> Should but shoulder Thee aside?

"A Canticle to the Christ in the Holy Eucharist" translates the meditation into graphic imagery: the doe seized by the buck's wounding love on the slopes of Tamalpais, the woman-shaped mountain north of San Francisco:

> In my heart you were might. And thy word was the running of
> rain
> That rinses October. And the sweetwater spring in the rock.
> And the brook in the crevice.
> Thy word in my heart was the start of the buck that is sourced
> in the doe.
> Thy word was the milk that will be in her dugs, the stir of new
> life in them.
> You gazed. I stood barren for days, lay fallow for nights.
> Thy look was the movement of life, the milk in the young
> breasts of mothers.

However, by 1954 the stresses of the monastic life had dried up the inspiration, and it could resume again in 1957 only after a profound, shattering "breakthrough into the unconscious" the previous year, made possible by Antoninus' association with the Dominican Jungian Victor White, and by saturating himself in archetypal psychology. The result was a long narrative poem called *River-Root*, which is the most sustained orgasmic celebration in English, perhaps in all literature. Amongst the Antoninus poems collected into *The Veritable Years*, *River-Root* can be seen as a watershed: the turning away from the often austere asceticism of the years just after conversion back down again to primal nature, now transfigured in the mystery of the Incarnation. The narrative objectivity of the poem permitted Antoninus, while still under the vow of chastity, to render the intercourse between the husband and wife with a candor that, far from detracting from its sacramentality, climaxes in a vision of the Trinity. God's entry into flesh locates the sexual mystery, its source and activity and end, in the very Godhead.

River-Root, then, represented at once a recovery and synthesis and turning point. It opened the way back to poetry—and to the world. In *The Hazards of Holiness* the ascetic Antoninus struggled with and against the drift that had already begun to carry him, unaware, back to Everson. The last section of that divided volume expresses the full range of his experience of the feminine archetype: from the sexual force leading men to their death in the title poem (whether demonically, like Salome and the Baptist, or heroically, like Judith and Holofernes) to the Virgin mother and spiritual Wisdom of "A Canticle to the Great Mother of God."

Two crucial poems here state the paradox in personal terms. "The Song the Body Dreamed in the Spirit's Mad Behest" extends the erotic imagery of bride and bridegroom from *The Canticle of Canticles* to depict the plunge of God into corporeal existence in blunt sexual expression possible only after Freud and Jung in this century and possible for Antoninus only through access to the unconscious:

> He is the Spirit but I am the Flesh.
> Our of my body must He be reborn,
> Soul from the sundered soul, Creation's gout
> In the world's bourn.
>
> Mounted between the thermals of my thighs
> Hawklike He hovers surging at the sun,
> And feathers me a frenzy ringed around
> That deep drunk tongue.

And the counterthrust of the Incarnation lifts our straining sexuality until we too are reborn, borne at last to Godhead:

> Proving what instinct sobs of total quest
> When shapeless thunder stretches into life,
> And the Spirit, bleeding, rears to overreach
> The buttocks' strife.
>
> .   .   .   .
>
> Born and reborn we will be groped, be clenched
> On ecstasies that shudder toward crude birth,

When his great Godhead peels its stripping strength
In my red earth.

"God Germed in Raw Granite" spells out the same reciprocating
movement: God descending into the curves and folds of the female
landscape; thence the "woman within" awakening the man erotically to
the call of Spirit; and finally the synthesis of masculine and feminine
twinned into a trinity by and with God:

I am dazed,
Is this she? Woman within!
Can this be? Do we, His images, float
Time-spun on that vaster drag
His timelessness evokes?
In the blind heart's core, when we
Well-wedded merge, by Him
Twained into one and solved there,
Are these still three? Are three
So oned, in the full-forthing
(Heart's reft, the spirit's great
Unreckonable grope, and God's
Devouring splendor in the stroke) are we—
This all, this utterness, this terrible
Total truth—indubitably He?

Could "she" remain merely the "woman within," the Anima arousing
the monk to rapturous response to God? For if he is to find God not in
some disembodied heaven but in the crucible of the heart, must he not run
the risks, trusting in Him Whom the unconscious aches to disclose, and
the passions burn to attain? "In Savage Wastes," the concluding poem of
Hazards, makes the decision to reenter the world; the way out of agonized
self-absorption, like the way out of pantheism, was "the more permeable
human context."

The Rose of Solitude tells of an encounter which moved him to his most
exalted realization of the Feminine. The highest recognition that I can give
the book, the final validation of poetry which refuses to distinguish
between art and life, is the fact that it will leave the reader, too, shaken and
transformed. The plot is not remarkable: Antoninus falls in love with a
Mexican-American woman, breaks his vow of chastity with her, is led by
her to repentance and confession; in the end they part. The remarkable
quality stems from the character of the Rose herself. The sequence
gradually reveals her and extols her as the apotheosis of the Feminine.
Beyond the divisions which split body from soul, beyond the mental

abstractions which man invents to cope ineffectually with those divisions, beyond his pity and self-pity, his hesitations, and recriminations, she emerges—all presence and act, all physical and spiritual beauty in one—spontaneous yet resting in herself, drawing him not by her will but by her being what she is. The sequence is so densely and intricately woven that it is difficult to excerpt passages, but "The Canticle of the Rose," "The Rose of Solitude" and "The Raging of the Rose" are prodigious feats of rhetoric, the poet pitching language to the extremes of articulation (the prolonged compounding of multisyllabic philosophical concepts in the "Canticle"; the wild incantation and imagery of "Solitude"; the synthesizing of the two modes in "Raging") in order to express the inexpressible fact that, in her, sexual sin becomes *felix culpa* and the Incarnation is accomplished. Accomplished in her, and, through his realization of her, in himself, "The Raging of the Rose" concludes with an affirmation of Selfhood sourced in the "I Am Who Am" of Genesis:

> Rose!
> Reality unfolded!
>
> On the four wings of the Cross,
> In the ecstasy of crucifixtion,
> In the blood of being,
> In the single burn of beauty
>
> BE!
>
> So that
> In you,
> The consummate
> Vision of Other:
>
> In you
> I AM!

But the relationship ends in separation: the monk returning to his cell, releasing her to her own life and to another relationship. The end of the book is muted—necessarily so, since the Rose has had to be experienced, for all her glory, as forbidden, alien finally to his chosen existence.

*

Thus, after all the years as Brother Antoninus, he still had not recovered, except in exalted moments, that unquestioned oneness which he had felt with nature in the mid-thirties. During the War his refusal of the Shadow-role of warrior had cast him, reciprocally, in a Shadow-relationship with the patriarchal institutions which said that he should fight. In middle age his commitment to the monastic ideal had made him similarily ambivalent about "the woman within," though she was the source of his religious experience as well as his Muse.

It could be no simple duality. Everson had experienced Christianity "as a Dionysian phenomenon" at the time of his conversion and in subsequent moments of mystical transcendence; and, as he later recalled it, "this same movement took me into the monastery—to exclude everything from the ecstatic Dionysian core" in the life of Brother Antoninus. Dionysus symbolizes the Anima-dominated man, whose creative energy comes from his feminine affinities. In the myth Dionysus' opponent is Pentheus, the repressive law-giver, the chaste soldier-king. Dionysus is Pentheus' Shadow, but is it not true that Penthus is Dionysus' Shadow as well, driving him to furious reprisals? What, then, of Everson and Antoninus? The situation is different because Antoninus is not Pentheus any more than Everson is simply Dionysus. If Everson and Antoninus are Shadows to each other, they are needed so within the single personality. Between them, even if we can distinguish twin aspects of the living person, lies no fight to the death, as with Pentheus and Dionysus, but a grappling toward accommodation, begun long before Everson became Antoninus. "The Sides of a Mind" in the late thirties is only one testimonial to how generic the struggle has been.

Thus, as psychic entity, the formative "Antoninus" had embodied a reflective, scrupulous, perfectionist dimension of character which got voiced in the earlier work mostly in his concern for revision and crafted statement. Later the monastically realized "Antoninus" brought to the work an emotional spiritual clarity and an intellectual subtlety that made for the most powerfully achieved poems. Hence "Antoninus," whether craftsman or monk, was no extraneous imposition but constituted an inherent reality. As Everson's becoming Antoninus represented an extension and integration of identity, not a denial, so his departure from the monastery would not affect the alchemy of his character.

Still, the tension persisted. He could be a Dionysian Christian, but could he remain a Dionysian monk? In the late sixties he moved toward taking final vows, even while sounding more emphatically the erotic basis of spirituality. *Who Is She That Looketh Forth as the Morning* redresses the previous image of Mary as Wisdom in "A Canticle to the Great Mother of God" by retrieving for her, at the moment of conception by the Spirit, the erotic and chthonic powers of a goddess like Venus. *Tendril in the Mesh*, Antoninus' last poem as a monk, strives to assimilate and terminate another love-relationship with a woman by subsuming its graphic sexual details in an "Epilogue" which experiences Incarnation not as idealized humanity but as animistic totem:

> Dark God of Eros, Christ of the buried brood,
> Stone-channelled beast of ecstasy and fire,
> The angelic wisdom in the serpentine desire,
> Fang hidden in the flesh's velvet hood
> Riddling with delight its visionary good.

After the first public reading of this poem in December, 1969, Brother Antoninus stripped off his religious habit and announced to his shocked audience that he was leaving the Dominican Order. Shortly thereafter he married, first outside the Church and later in the Church, Susanna Rickson, to whom *Tendril* is dedicated. They live near Santa Cruz, where Everson teaches at the University of California.

*

The precipitate departure indicated how much like a thunderclap it came, even to himself; and the poems of *Man-Fate* (1974) are the words of a man caught in a psychic crossfire: Antoninus become Everson again. During the years as Brother Antoninus, nature had remained a strong religious presence for him. The elegy for Jeffers, *The Poet is Dead*, works almost completely through images of the California coast, and poems like "The South Coast," "A Canticle to the Waterbirds," and "In All These Acts" project pantheism into Christian mystery. Now Everson withdrew again to nature to validate his break with Antoninus, but with a consciousness heightened and complicated by all that Antoninus had come to realize and value, and by the monastery life that Everson found it excruciating to leave behind. In the opacities of the elemental matrix he would be healed or torn apart.

That venture into the primeval is enacted in a sequence of dreams and archetypal fantasies which comprise the climax of *Man-fate*. In "The Narrows of Birth," on Christmas night, twenty-one years after his conversion experience, he dreams of joining the clan gathered around the Great Mother of Nature. He bows before her for absolution, but instead sees her followers begin the castration of a young man, whose body is "slumped in its unmistakably erotic swoon." The dreamer finds the Great Mother betraying him to join in the castration. The dream in "The Black Hills" shows Everson fighting his way back in psychic as well as historical time to recover the Indians in all their splendid strength, and to seek the blessing of his dark, dead Father, whom he loves and whom civilization taught him to dread and kill. All but overwhelmed in the furious rush of the braves, he cannot wring a word of recognition from the chief. In the aftermath of the dream he rises briefly to conscious acquiescence in the natural round, which the red men honored and the white men violated: "All Indian at last,/ I lift up my arms and pray"; but even that moment is broken off anti-climactically.

The nightmares tell what Antoninus already knew: that one cannot give over to the Shadow; abandonment to the powers of darkness without a guide will end in dissolution, chaos, death. For the man, the Anima can be such a mediator. She is grounded in the Shadow-area so strongly that at times she seems merely his vassal and instrument: the Feminine as temptation or threat. But in coping with the Shadow the man also engages *her*. And if trusted and loved, she can free him from enslavement to the Shadow, mediating the unconscious and the passions, drawing them from blind automation into activity and actualization in masculine consciousness, and thus opening the way gradually to Selfhood: the apocalypse of the polarized personality into androgynous, undivided identity. The Self is the psychological equivalent of the Beatific Vision, glimpsed in our supreme moments, but mostly striven for through the polar rhythms of living. For in Selfhood the individual attains not just what is uniquely himself, but thereby attains participation in the Godhead in which we shall all find ourselves at last.

Under the onslaught of the Shadow in *Man-Fate* Everson's response is instinctive and right: he turns to touch his wife. She is the objective verification of the Anima: a somnolent but locating presence, waiting for his return from lonely contention with the Shadow. For after the powerful consolidation of the Anima in *The Rose* and the subsequent poems, now no longer alien and suspect but tallied in his marriage, she lies ready to wake again from drowsy abeyance to spring him into the next thrust towards Selfhood. The last words of the book are:

> I have made a long run.
> I have swum dark waters.
>
> I have followed you through hanging traps.
> I have risked it all.
>
> O cut my thongs!
>
> At the fork of your flesh
> Our two trails come together.
>
> At your body's bench
> I take meat.

Expressed in the archetypal terms of the human psyche, the Incarnation is God entering into, permeating and operating through the Feminine, just as the Annunciation proclaims. The concluding image above, physical yet suggestive of the sacramental act, constitutes, more immediately and elementally than with the Rose, the personalizing of the regenerative, redemptive mystery in the witness of the wife to the power of the Anima. Mother and wife and priestess in one, she administers him nourishment needed now for the way ahead.

Printed August 1978 in Santa Barbara & Ann Arbor
for the Black Sparrow Press by Mackintosh and Young
& Edwards Brothers Inc. Design by Barbara Martin.
This edition is published in paper wrappers; there
are 500 hardcover trade copies; 250 hardcover copies
have been numbered & signed by the author;
& there are 50 copies handbound in boards by
Earle Gray, each containing a holograph poem by
William Everson.

photo: Ron Chamberlain

William Everson was born in 1912 at Sacramento, California, and grew up in the San Joaquin Valley. He attended Fresno State College where he encountered the verse of Robinson Jeffers, crystalizing his own vocation as a poet. In World War II he served as a conscientious objector, then returned to the Bay Area to join the group of poets around Kenneth Rexroth, nucleus of the famed San Francisco Renaissance. In 1949 he converted to Catholicism and in 1951 entered the Dominican Order, taking the name of Brother Antoninus. In 1969, after eighteen years as a lay brother, he left the Dominicans to marry. He lives in the mountains with his wife and son near the University of California at Santa Cruz, where he is poet in residence. He has published over forty volumes of poetry and scholarship, and is a handpress printer of distinction. His honors include a Guggenheim Fellowship in 1949, the Commonwealth Club of California's Silver Medal in 1967, and co-winner of the Shelley Memorial Award in 1968.